Super
Working Mum

Living and Loving Life To The Fullest

Aloted Omoba

Aloted Inc Limited

First published in 2014 by
Aloted Inc Limited
75 Lancaster Road Essex RM16 6EA

Super Working Mum
© 2014 Aloted Omoba

Book Cover designed by Leanne Kelly
Book layout by Esho Olatokunbo

ISBN: 978-0-9561484-14

Printed in the United Kingdom

praise for Super Working Mum

What a joy it is to know Aloted; she is most certainly gifted and the Lord is using her mightily to truly bless women. This book has some quite outstanding wisdom and practical Godly help for our everyday lives. You will be inspired, uplifted and excited about your future as you read how to improve and make adjustments to begin to live the life you have always dreamed of. This book is surely God given.

~Fiona Hendley Jones, Evangelist and encourager to the body of Christ.

Are you a woman whose aim is to reach greater heights while balancing family, career, business and passion? Then this book is a must have in your arsenal of weapons. Aloted Omoba breaks down useful tips, tools and techniques that will help today's woman to reach their highest potential, while serving a super natural God. The conversational tone of each page gives you a warm and fuzzy feeling like you are talking to your best friend and will keep you turning the pages for more. Learn to love and live your life to the fullest with real life experiences that are wrapped in a blanket of humor.

~Unoma Nwankwor, Christian Fiction Author and Publisher at KevStel Group

There are a lot of books out there for working mums but what sets this one apart is the approach. Aloted isn't just talking fluff; she's sharing real-world advice from her experience and the experience of those who've been there in order to help you learn from their combined wisdom. Don't pass it by. Super Working Mum is a vital resource that can be put into practice immediately.

~Aji R. Michael, Leadership Coach and Author of The Next Maverick: Ready to Shape the Future

Aloted has done an excellent job in this practical guide to becoming a Super Working Mum. Inspiration is woven throughout the fabric of the book and you are left not only better informed, but also very refreshed by her honesty and candour.

**~Toks Aruoture, Writer and
Baby & Children's Interior Designer, Punkin Patch Interiors**

praise for Boosting Your Confidence

Boosting Your Confidence, by Aloted is an eye-opener and enlightening ebook that will give the reader a new perspective to dealing with, every day life challenges and obstacles in the pursuit of success, contentment and fulfillment.

~Seun Rominiyi, Professional accountant and Inspirational writer, UK

I believe there's always room for improvement and change. I recommend Boosting Your Confidence to everyone who wants to improve some aspect of their life."

~Tolu Popoola, Writer, Publisher and Blogger at onwritingandlife.com

I read Boosting Your Confidence quite easily in about 30 minutes (which is always a plus for me!) and there are a number of points which I definitely will try out and hope to practice regularly to boost my confidence even more"

~Tola Omoniyi, SEO Analyst and Blogger at callmemummy.com

testimonials

Aloted! You are the Best! Thank you for helping me get my year off to a great start! You are so great and responsive to all my needs and questions! I am so grateful for your help in growing my business!

~Marcella Kerwin, Founder of Boot Camp LA and Happy Healthy Fit Girls!

Aloted has a very natural manner while teaching you practical business ideas that you can easily implement, saving you time & effort. I would highly recommend her courses as a working mum of six.

~Michelle Williams, Founder Shelby Art Mentoring

Aloted has completely understood and helped work miracles in the beginning steps of my business journey. She was able to give me the small simple steps I needed and could follow. Aloted is a great teacher and I look forward to learning more!"

~Pennie Rumsey, Founder Path of Providence

I love the Super Working Mum group. Keep up the good work Aloted, motivating, encouraging and empowering women to do the best they possibly can.

~Toyin Empress-Adeleye

I'm thanking God for this wonderful group, Super Working Mum. The knowledge we share is priceless. Sometimes just knowing that there are women all over the world going through stuff same as me is so comforting. Much love, Aloted.

~Brownie Owolabi, Founder Deborahs Kitchen

dedication

I dedicate this book to all the Super Working Mums
endeavouring to grow their faith, whilst managing a home,
and holding down a job at the same time.

You are doing an awesome job!

acknowledgment

I thank God for the wisdom, strength, and inspiration to start Super Working Mum, and to write this book. Without God, I am nothing.

To my darling husband, Tj, thank you for your unwavering support and patience, for challenging me to dream big, and for being my biggest cheerleader.

To my Dad and Mum, thank you for bringing me up in the way of the Lord. Because of this, I am fulfilling my purpose on earth.

A big shout out to the mastermind group I am a part of- Diane Ore, Chichi Eruchalu, Emilia Newman, Rice and Justina Rosu, for your creativity, support, and wisdom. You ladies are just super.

To my Inner Circle Ladies, thank you for allowing me be of service to you. You make the Super Working Mum journey worthwhile.

Uncle Gboyega Eyitayo, I am forever grateful to you, for recognising and telling me at the age of eight that I had the gift of writing.

Thank you, my dear friend, Ronke Odewumi, for believing in me, and helping me rediscover my gift of writing and helping women.

Funmi Onamusi and Atilola Moronfolu, I am grateful for the several crash courses on self publishing and printing the book.

To all my friends, loved ones and supporters, for your encouraging words and emails, I am thankful. God bless you all.

table of content

foreword

What a wonderful 'Tool-kit' for the working woman and mother! Why do I say so? You know your typical handy-man box of tools men usually have in the garage or work shed, the one with tools of different shapes fabricated to tackle nuts and bolt of varying sizes? This book you now hold in your hand is very much like that handy box of tools because in these pages, I believe you will find a 'tool' to tackle every 'nutty' issue of life you might face as a woman, wife and mother.

From self-care tips to anger management tips to how to cultivate an attitude of gratitude to how to remember birthdays to keeping the flames sizzling in your marriage, Aloted covers it all and more! She has, based on her own life's experiences till date, put together a treasure trove of wisdom for the ordinary woman who seeks to live an extraordinary life at work and at home.

Motivational and inspirational books of this nature can be tricky. You want to help but you don't want to come off sounding like a know-it-all, or condescending. There is a fine balance to watch, and I believe Aloted has managed that balance well. She sincerely wants you to be the best all-round person, wife, and mum you can be, and it comes through in her words, which are always rooted in the Word of God.

One of personal favorites is 'You Don't Have to Catch the Ball' because it really reminded me of my newly-married self, and how I went all out to prove that I was the best wife, home-maker, cook, sex kitten, and in-law in the entire universe! If there was a 'Martha Stewart' prize, I wanted to win it! Sadly, it took me over seven years to realise that my husband had only two basic needs, and as long as I was 'catching those balls', all was good in the hood, *smiling*. Now, why do you have to learn the hard way like me when you can read this book, get your 'wisdom on' now, and save yourself all the hassle?

At the end of the day, life's issues are universal. So, all women are the same to the extent that we go through more or less the same things, albeit at different times, and in different ways. In this book, Aloted seeks to share with you her many 'secrets' to living above the mediocre line. She wants you to live victoriously NOW! She does not want you to be just a working mum. Aloted wants you to be better than that. She wants you to be a Super Working Mum! Yes, a mum bringing up the next generation empowered by a Supernatural God!

I honestly believe that every woman should read this book. You don't have to be married neither do you have to be a mum yet. There is a wealth of wisdom here that has the potential to transform your life should you begin to apply it to your everyday living.

Read with an open heart. It is my prayer that as you do, the spirit of love behind Aloted's words will move over your life and transform you, day by day, into the supernaturally empowered working mum God destined you to be!

In God's love and mine,
Bola 'Salt' Essien-Nelson
abimbolaen@yahoo.com

introduction

Faith, Family, and Work are the three most integral parts of my life, and juggling them all can sometimes be overwhelming.

As a single lady working for Accenture, one of the top consulting firms in the world, travelling from city to city and practically living out of my suitcase was the highlight of my life. It was an absolute joy! I later got married, and things changed a bit. However, the BIG change occurred when I gave birth to my daughter.

All of a sudden, my schedule and priorities changed. I suddenly became responsible for another human's existence. It was a whole new experience, and it seemed nerve-racking at first. It still can be! However, I knew I had to find a way to adapt to this drastic change in my life.

I began to trust God more, research, learn, and implement strategies that helped me cope with prioritising and combining my work and home duties effortlessly. Super Working Mum was therefore born out of my desire to share my findings with other working mums.

By the time my son was born, my life had taken a whole new

turn. I was no longer the career-driven girl I used to be. The top items on my list of priority had become getting closer to God, taking care of my family, and using my writing and teaching gift to help other working mums know they can be super, by trusting in the supernatural power of God.

I have therefore put my top practical tips in an easy-to-read book that can be accessible worldwide by mums in need of help in all aspects of their lives.

This book provides tools, strategies, and practical tips for working mums, including those in business, who want to excel at work, and still be outstanding women.

This book is for every mum, whether working or not. Most of the tips and strategies provided in this book emanate from my Christian faith, but I believe that regardless of your belief system, you will find most of the tips I provide, practical and beneficial.

Please, note that the advice in this book is not coming from a woman who has it all together, or is under the illusion that she is perfect. I am actually an everyday person who has either dealt with, or is currently dealing with most of the issues and challenges raised in this book.

The Super Working Mum journey is one of excellence, and not of perfection, which is what this book reflects, and I would like you to embark on this journey with me. By applying the principles I share, I believe that though your life may not be perfect, you will be more fulfilled, and find more balance in your life.

I hope you are blessed by it.

Blessings,
Aloted

YOU ARE BEAUTIFUL

This is a shout out to every Super Working Mum

You are beautifully-crafted by God
You can do anything you set your mind to do
You are the best wife for your husband
You are the best mum for your children
You are the best woman for your role at work
You are selfless
You are kind
You are worth more than you can imagine
You are unique and special
You are someone to reckon and associate with
You deserve appreciation and praise
You are a woman of influence
You are stronger than you know
You overcome challenges and difficulties
You make a difference in people's lives
You have talents and gifts
You are awesome
You have SUPER special abilities- you create, you nurture,
and you bring to birth.

So believe in yourself; I believe in YOU

Give yourself some credit. If you don't, nobody else will!

Celebrate your success as a woman, wife, and mother.

Make decisions, and act on them, CONFIDENTLY.

Don't be afraid to try out new things.

Because guess what….

God's got you!

Never forget that.

MY PRAYER FOR YOU

To all the Super Working Women reading this book, this is my prayer for you.

If you are trying to conceive- I pray you will conceive, carry, and deliver your own baby safely.

If you are pregnant- I pray for a supernatural childbirth.

If your marriage is in trouble- I pray for peace and restoration of love.

If you are looking for a job- I pray you will get the job your heart desires, according to God's Will.

If you are on a career path- I pray for promotion in your career.

If you are in business- I pray for favour, right paying customers, and success in your business.

If you are sick or have a sick family member- I pray for complete healing.

If you are unhappy or troubled- I pray for joy in your life, and God's peace that surpasses all understanding.

If you are in a financial difficulty - I pray for financial breakthrough.

If you are experiencing any type of loss- I pray for the comfort and peace of the Holy Spirit.

If you are confused about the path to take- I pray for divine direction, wisdom, and clarity on what to do.

If you are afraid- I pray for sound mind, power, and courage.

If you are in need- I pray God meets you at the point of your need, according to His will for you.

…In Jesus Name.

Simply believe!

WHO IS A SUPER WORKING MUM?

Is the Super Working Mum (SWM) a myth? Does this woman even exist?

A Super Working Mum is a woman who depends solely on the supernatural power of God to become the woman He has called her to be, in every aspect of her life. She is on a journey to becoming exceptional in all her roles, not settling for mediocrity along the way. The term 'super' reflects excellence, not perfectionism. It refers to the power of God in us.

I know I am nowhere near being super, neither do I have it all together, but I am on a journey to becoming that woman. In order to become a SWM, I must see myself as God sees me, and affirm that to myself.

QUALITIES OF A SUPER WORKING MUM

The process of compiling this list required my in-depth thinking. It was inspired by a combination of the qualities of the Proverbs 31 woman, and the admirable traits I have seen in my own mother and other great mothers I know. They are in no particular order.

Home

A Super Working Mum

- is the CEO of her home
- takes good care of her family
- gets out of bed before everyone else
- manages the finances of her home, with her husband
- carries her husband along in the affairs of her home
- is observant of the needs of her family
- is gentle and patient with her family

Work

A Super Working Mum

- either has a job, business, or an income-generating hobby
- conducts herself with professionalism and integrity
- is diligent and confident at her work place or business
- is assertive

Lifestyle

A Super Working Mum

- reads books that edify her mentally and spiritually
- has a simplified and organised life
- influences people with her a positive attitude
- is conscious of what she eats, and keeps fit
- is financially-savvy, and can manage money well
- looks good, takes care of herself, and dresses for her

body type

Attitude

A Super Working Mum

- · has a good sense of humour
- · does not take herself or life too seriously
- · is aware of her strengths and weaknesses
- · enhances her strengths, and places less emphasis on her weaknesses
- · is not afraid of change
- · is not afraid to make mistakes, but learns from them
- · is strong, confident, and in control of her emotions

Relationships

A Super Working Mum

- · puts God first and in the centre of her life
- · is spiritually, mentally, emotionally, and physically mature
- · has a great relationship with her husband, if married
- · loves and disciplines her children
- · chooses her friends wisely
- · is a role model to other women who want to be super as well, is willing and available to help them

General

A Super Working Mum

- knows how to prioritise, and is in charge of her time
- is aware of her stress-triggers, and manages stress well
- is not defined by her work or her role as a mum, but secured in her identity in God
- is a great planner, and result-oriented
- knows she is doing her best, and lets the rest go
- knows she can't do it all, asks for help, and is not afraid to delegate
- does not micromanage

My goal is to take one quality on this list at a time, work on it, and move on to the next.

Please, note that this list is not cast in stone. Your list could be similar or different, depending on your perspective and personality. Why don't you go ahead, and create your list?

Studies have shown that you are more likely to succeed in achieving your goals when you have support. We provide support in our Faith, Family and Financial Freedom Inner Circle, for mums who want to become super in every aspect of their lives. Will you join me in this journey?

Scan this QR code using your smart phone
or go to http://bit.ly/swm-fff
to find out how to join the Faith, Family
and Financial Freedom Inner Circle

NURTURE YOUR SPIRIT MAN

You have probably heard that you are a spirit, who lives in a body, and have a soul. The REAL you is your spirit man, who simply lives in an earthly body. Therefore, it is imperative that your spirit man is nurtured and developed, so you can hear from God on a daily basis.

Many mothers focus on physical exercise to lose weight, and tone their muscles. Whilst this is good, it is more important to focus on exercising your spiritual muscles. This will enable you live on a supernatural level, and in God's strength.

We can only develop a solid relationship with God through our spirit man. He speaks to us through our spirit. Our spiritual ears therefore, need to be sensitive enough to hear what He is saying at all times.

I have noticed that the mornings I get up to spend time with God, worshipping, meditating, and praying, I usually experience a calmer and more peaceful day. This doesn't mean challenges don't come my way, but I am usually more equipped to deal with issues more appropriately, in God's power.

If you keep living your life without relating to your heavenly father on a daily basis, staying plugged in to Him, and nurturing your spirit man, you will eventually run on empty. It is only a matter of time before you burn out and become overwhelmed by life's challenges. If your foundation is shaky, it will affect every other aspect of your life.

There are several ways to develop your spirit man, but the most important step is to intentionally start every day with God. Learn to connect with Him in prayer, meditation, and by reading the Bible.

Being surrounded by, and connecting with other people who desire to grow in their faith, is also a great way to nurture your spirit man. Being a member of a Bible-believing church is also paramount.

Be careful of what you watch, read, or listen to. I believe that the more you feed your spirit, the less you will desire to feed your flesh. This may seem like a tall order, but if you truly desire to live a supernatural life, and get the wisdom you need to make right decisions, you have to do what it takes. Take it one day at a time, and trust in God to help you.

So what are you going to do differently from today, to develop your spirit man?

WORK-LIFE VISION

As a Super Working Mum, you must have a vision for your life.

"Where there is no vision [no redemptive revelation of God], the people perish." Prov 29:18 (AMP)

Without a vision, your life will have no direction, and you will constantly react to emergencies of life, as opposed to living a purposeful life.

Since you became a mum, have your dreams suddenly taken the back seat? Has the vision God given you suddenly evaporated into thin air? It is a great privilege and blessing to be a mum, but to live a purposeful life, you have to stop putting yourself last, and start moving in the direction of your vision.

One day, your children will grow up, leave home, and move on with their lives. Will you gladly welcome that period of inevitable change, or will you desperately want to hold on to your children, because they have become your identity?

The key is in learning how to balance being a mum with not losing your identity in the process. This is where your work-life vision comes in. If you fail to plan, you are planning to fail. Having a work-life vision will help you know if you are heading in the right direction or not. It is like laying a critical foundation for your life and that of your family.

Many women have a vague plan and idea of where they want to be in five years in their career, work, or business, but sadly, not many can say this about their personal lives.

WHY SHOULD YOU HAVE A VISION?

A vision:
- gets you up in the morning because you have something meaningful you have set out to do
- gives you a sense of direction
- helps you balance your priorities, and decide what is important
- gives your life meaning and purpose
- gives you focus and direction, and helps you make decisions in your family and personal life
- gets you through days when you face opposition or criticism from others
- helps you retain self-motivation, gives you energy, and gets you going

"Lack of direction, not lack of time is the problem. We all have 24 hours in the day." - Zig Ziglar

If you have a vision, your days will be filled with purpose and working on your priorities, so that you can ultimately achieve your God-given vision.

Below are some steps on how to create a work-life vision, based on a combination of my thoughts and what I read in Michael Hyatt's book, Creating Your Personal Life Plan. You will need to write out your vision on paper, as there is power in the written word.

"…Write the vision and make it plain on tablets…" Hab 2:2 (NIV)

HOW DO YOU WANT TO BE REMEMBERED?

This exercise below might seem gloomy and melancholic, but it is something I want you to do.

Imagine your burial ceremony. You are lying in your coffin. Your family, friends, colleagues, and business associates are all in attendance. Everyone is talking about your life. What are they saying about you?

This is an extremely important question. To be able to answer it, you have to fast-forward to the end of your life, and look back. When you leave this earth, you leave behind the memories you created, and the impact you had on the lives of others. I know this sounds very morbid, but remember life is short, and this earth is not our home.

If you know the conversations people will have about you after you die is nothing you would be proud of, begin to make little changes today to channel the direction of that conversation in the way you want it to go.

SET YOUR PRIORITIES

Decide who or what is important to you.

My top priorities are - God, myself (health, personal growth, and rest), my husband, my children, my relationships, and my work. Your priorities could be similar to, or completely different from mine, since we are all different.

In my list, God comes first, because without Him in the centre, everything will fall apart. Therefore, spending time with Him, and meditating on His words in the Bible are very important to me.

After God, comes myself. Even though it might seem selfish, it is not really the case. A lot of mums are busy taking care of others, while they keep pushing their own needs to the bottom of the list. The truth is, if I don't take care of myself, i.e. my spiritual, mental, and emotional needs, I would not be able to take care of my family, and serve others more effectively. With this, I am also setting a good example to my children that it is okay for them to take care of themselves.

After myself, my husband comes next. It is very easy to lump my husband and children together, but I make a conscious effort not to. Your husband should have a higher priority over your children. When your children are long gone, your husband would be the only one left with you. He, not your children, is your partner, and both of you should form a formidable team. When children observe the strong relationship between their parents, it boosts their confidence, and also keeps them grounded.

Once your husband has been taken care of, the children can then come into the mix. Sometimes I push my family to the bottom of the list, and even put work before them, which eventually makes me feel guilty. I always have to consciously make an effort to be present with my children, when I am with them.

Do you also struggle in this aspect too? To solve this problem, if you work in an office, don't take work home. If you work from home, when you are with your children, give them your whole attention, and don't get distracted by the laptop or phone.

Your relationship with people should also be a top priority. Value it over material things. Having a solid support system will help you a great deal. Aim to always have a positive impact on people. Let kindness be your watchword. Appreciate your friends and loved ones. Help others even when it is not convenient. Aim to be the biggest giver in all your relationships. You might not always achieve this, but at least, you will develop an attitude of giving.

Your job can be a rewarding experience if you do not let it become your idol. However, if you don't put it in its place, it can suck the life out of you. No one ever said at the end of their life, "I only wish I had spent more time at work." A lot of people sacrifice their time with God and family for their jobs. Don't let this be said of you.

After all said, your job is still important. Decide how many hours you want to work in a week. Does your current working environment allow you put your family first? If no, it may be time for a change.

Are you fulfilled where you are working? Do you want to start a business? What is important to you?

Continue to work on your priority list, by asking yourself what is important, and why it is. Some of them may be interchangeable, but I believe the first four in your life should always be God, you, your spouse, and your children.

Being realistic, sometimes I mix up my priorities, by doing things such as putting God last, myself at the bottom of the list, or my job before my family. However, by writing out my priorities, I become more conscious of what I need to do, and work towards it.

CREATE YOUR VISION ACTION PLAN

I am a business analyst by profession, and one of the things we do when analysing a business process is to outline the As-Is process, i.e. the current situation. After that, we outline what the To-Be process should look like i.e. how we want the situation to be in future. After doing this, we perform a Gap Analysis, to identify the gaps between both scenarios. We then outline the action steps the business needs to take, in order to move from the As-Is to the To–Be stage.

This type of analysis can also be applied in every area of our lives. Pick each area you wrote in your priority list, and write down what exactly your current situation is. Be honest, but don't over analyse. Just write whatever comes to your mind, both positives and the negatives. The aim is not to make you feel bad if your priorities are currently misplaced, but to help you see what areas you need to improve on.

The next step is to ignore your current situation for a moment, and write what you desire to see in those areas. Write them in the present tense, as if they are already a reality.

Lastly, compare your current reality to your desired projection, and identify the gaps. Write down the steps you need to take to move from where you are to where you want to be.

This should constitute your work-life vision plan. You will need to schedule a regular time to review your plan, and determine whether you are making progress or not. Get your spouse on board if possible, so it would be a joint effort, and you would not be working in isolation.

By creating a work-life vision, you will start to live a purpose-driven life. Try it, and see.

CAN I HAVE IT ALL?

Maintaining a healthy work-family balance is one concern almost every working mum I know has. You are probably concerned about this as well.

Can you have it all? My opinion is that motherhood and parenting is a large part of who you are as a woman, and this will have an effect on every other aspect of your life.

Oprah Winfrey once said, ***"You can have it all, not just all at once."*** I agree with her. I also read somewhere that between work, family, and marriage, a woman must choose TWO to succeed at, or fail at all three.

I personally think every Super Working Mum can avoid failing at all three, by realising there is a time for everything. With a change in mind-set, adopting a degree of flexibility, and strategising, you can have it all, whatever 'all' means to you.

DITCH THE WORKING MUM GUILT

First of all, you need to ditch the Working Mum guilt. I believe you are working for a good reason, and currently doing your best to care for your family. Drowning in guilt will not improve the situation; this is your current reality. You can either choose to continually get depressed by it, or change it.

What you need to do is set some boundaries. When you are at work, focus on work. When you are at home, focus on your children. If you work from home, have a set time where you shut down your job, and switch to mummy role.

Also, if you have your work-life vision in place, and understand why you are working, guilt will have no hold on you.

WHAT CHANGES CAN YOU MAKE?

Take a step back, assess your current situation, and determine what you can change about it. At this point in your life, what is important to you?

If your work is not allowing you spend time with your children, and this makes you unhappy, what can you do to achieve some work-family balance?

- Can you change your job to a less-strenuous one?
- Can you ask for flexible working hours, or fewer hours at your place of work?

- Can you start a work-from-home business?
- Can you reduce your business hours?

Change is one of the hardest things in life. Moving from something that is certain to uncertainty takes COURAGE. It will cost you, but the good news is that you will gain much more.

MONEY ISN'T EVERYTHING

You may ask yourself how you will cope with less income if you reduce your hours at work, take a less-paying job, or reduce your business hours. I had the same worry when I changed jobs some years ago, in order to spend more time with my daughter. I got a pay cut when I changed jobs, because I decided to work somewhere local, rather than the city. However, I understood that money isn't everything.

The question I asked myself was "what is the point of having all the money in the world, at the risk of losing a great relationship with my daughter?"

A pay cut may require a change in lifestyle and spending habits. If it has to come to this, consider the questions below.

- What can you do without?

- In what ways can you spend less?
- How can you save money?

Being CONTENT with what you have will help you live within your means, and avoid horrendous debts.

GET SOME SUPPORT

Get support from your spouse, if you are married, and most especially, from other working mums. This is not meant to disrespect anyone, but sometimes, your spouse may not understand the struggles you are dealing with as a working mum. Your spouse might advise you from his point of view, and I believe you appreciate this, but sometimes it is not enough to propel you.

I therefore suggest having a support network of other working mums who are like-minded, and also desire to achieve work-family balance. Encourage and share what works for you with one another. Knowing you are not alone in the struggle will help you a great deal.

DON'T COMPARE YOURSELF TO OTHER MUMS

You may see another mum doing it all, climbing the career ladder smoothly, driving the latest car, doing well in her business, living large, and to cap it up, her marriage and family look fantastic.

That's her, and this is you. As they say, the grass is always greener on the other side. Every mum's situation is different. You don't know what sacrifices she might have made in the past, or the details of her life.

Stay focused on yourself, your family, and vision. Comparing yourself to another mum would only depress you, and slow you down.

KEEP EVALUATING YOUR SITUATION

Keep in mind that this won't be your situation forever. When your children are older, or things get better, God will give you wisdom concerning the next step to take, if you ask Him.

The important thing is to take each day as it comes. You would have invested in the right things, and will reap the rewards in due season.

Who said being a working mum was easy?

DEVELOP YOUR GIFT!

Since you became a mother, have you suddenly given up on your dreams? Have you stopped using your God-given talents? Do you even remember what your gifts are?

Everyone has gifts, God made sure of that. However, some people tend to thrive and excel in the expression of their gifts more than others, because they have discovered how to develop their gifts. It is these people who tend to feel happier, more empowered, and more fulfilled.

Proverbs 18:16 says *"A (wo)man's gift makes room for her, and brings her before great men."* (KJV, paraphrased). This confirms that we all have gifts. We just have to use them, because this is what would open doors of opportunities for us.

Proverbs 22:29 also says *"Do you see a (wo)man who excels in her work? She will stand before kings; She will not stand before unknown men."* (NKJV, paraphrased)

This verse of the Bible tells us we have to develop our gifts, in order to stand before influential people! It is one thing to discover your gift, but another to work on it, be consumed by it, and excel in it. When you do this, people will begin to refer to you, you will be the answer to someone's problem, not just someone, but a GREAT person. They will look for you; you won't have to go looking for them. You have to be very good at your gift, such that when someone thinks of whom to call for help in your area of expertise, your name is the first to pop in their mind.

Understandably, it takes time to get to that level where you are known, but sadly, a lot of us give up before we even begin. The initial stage, which a friend of mine tagged as the 'silent years', would require you doing some researching, developing, learning, and working your gift.

A client of mine, whose plan is to start a business, told me she has been reading and researching a lot, but not taking practical steps in exercising of her gift. She felt she was wasting time, but I told her she was not. She is simply in the development and silent stage. It would take some time for her to work her gifts, and make her dreams a reality.

Have you ever heard of the 10, 000 hour rule? Malcolm Gladwell mentioned this rule in his book, Outliers: The Story of Success. The rule states that in order for an individual to master any complex skill, whether it is brain surgery, playing the cello, etc., he/she must put in 10,000 hours of focused practice. For instance, it would take ten years of practicing three hours a day to become a master at your subject. It would take you approximately five years of full-time employment to become proficient in your field.

This rule implies that the successful people you see today didn't suddenly get there. It took thousands of hours of practice and persistence. The more hours you invest in developing your gift, the better you will become at it. Just as they say, practice makes perfect.

As a side note to parents, once you discover your children's gift, hone it, and encourage them to start working on it immediately. This way, by the time they get older, they would have mastered it, and can excel at it.

As a mum, what do you enjoy doing? What are you passionate about? If you are not sure about it, ask God to show you. Ask your family and friends to tell you what they think you are good at. Once you have figured it out, start working that gift.

My gifts are writing and teaching, and I am now using my gifts to help other mums create a life and business they love, through my books, webinars, courses, etc. It took me a while to pinpoint my gifts, but I am now working on it, and loving it. I am using my gifts to bless others, to the glory of God, and it is such an amazing thing.

Don't let being a mum stop you from polishing your gift. Stop putting yourself last. I know it is easier said than done, but one day, your children would leave home. Then, what would you have left? It is high time you went back to the drawing board to learn, research, develop and work your gift(s). No more excuses.

When you leave this earth, and face God on judgement day, you would want to be able to stand tall and proud, knowing you made use of your gifts, rather than giving excuses about why you didn't exercise them.

Fear may want to stop you from realising your dreams, but remember God has not given you the spirit of fear, but of power, love, and a sound mind. Anytime I feel scared to use my gift, such as the time I was writing this book, I take my attention off my fears or insecurities, and focus on how others can be blessed through my gift. When I shift the focus from me to others, and think of how I can be of service and a blessing, fear gets no place in me to breed anymore.

Dear Super Working Mum, it is time to step out of your comfort zone, and take action. You have a unique gift waiting to be shared with the world. You are the solution to someone's problem. Go forth and develop that gift.

MAKE ME A BLESSING

Do you desire to be blessed by God? If so, one of the things you need to do is to be a blessing to others. It is that simple.

A friend once shared her testimony with me. She had applied for a new job, but felt led to pray for another lady who was also job-hunting. My friend went as far as sending the lady a job advertisement in her field. Eventually, the other lady got the job! Her friend expressed her appreciation by praying for my friend, and saying, "God bless you." That same week, my friend got the job she applied for, with fantastic perks accompanying it. It was indeed a miracle!

This is a universal law, which is also God's mathematics: what you sow, you reap.

The truth is every single one of us has problems, be it big, small, or medium-sized. Instead of throwing a pity party, believing your problem is the biggest of them all, and that you deserve special attention from God and everyone else, you should reach out to bless others instead. This attitude will definitely open doors for you.

The typical prayer a lot of us pray is "God bless me." It is high time we changed that prayer to "Lord, make me a blessing to others."

SOME PRACTICAL WAYS WE CAN BE A BLESSING TO OTHERS

- Do you want a promotion at work? Volunteer to mentor someone at your workplace, who needs help.
- Do you want your business to grow? Give support to a rookie in business, by sharing business tips and resources.
- Do you want a new job? As you do your job search, and come across job ads that don't quite match your preferences, forward them to someone you think might be interested.
- Do you want healing? Pray for someone else who is sick.
- Do you want a child? Rejoice with those who have children. Attend a friend's baby dedication with a gift, and offer to babysit for a friend who needs assistance.
- Do you want financial breakthrough? Give to someone in need.
- Do you want to buy a house? Pay towards someone's mortgage or rent.

How did God show us that He loves us? He GAVE! He gave his ONLY son to die for us. So if you say you love, you must GIVE. Give, and it will be given to you, says the Bible. Givers never lack. Give of your time, money, resources, knowledge, etc. When we bless others by giving, we are sowing seeds of abundance.

Please note that I am in no way suggesting that you give what you do not have. Deuteronomy 16:17 says *"Every man shall give as **he is able**, according to the blessing of the Lord your God which He has given you." (NKJV, with emphasis)*. Start with the little you have, not what you don't have.

Read God's promise to Abraham in Genesis 12:2 *"I will make you a great nation; I will bless you and make your name great; And you shall be a blessing." (NKJV)*. God will make you great, SO THAT you can be a blessing to others. Did I hear you say Amen?

Do you want to be blessed? Then change your attitude. Change your prayer to "Lord, make me a blessing." You will be surprised at the different opportunities life will present you, so you could be a blessing to others. Take advantage of those opportunities, and the reward that comes with being a blessing to others will flow your way.

WAITING ON GOD

Sometime ago, I was talking with a group of ladies, and the conversation steered towards how hard it is to wait for anything. One of the ladies then asked this question. "Is it easier to wait on God for a husband or a baby?"

A single lady in the group quickly answered "Oh, it is definitely harder to wait for a husband than a baby. At least, a childless married woman has one out of the two, while the single lady has neither." A few other ladies nodded their heads in agreement.

A married woman in the group then countered the single lady's opinion by saying "No, I think it is harder waiting for a baby. There are numerous single men around, and you can easily pick one to marry, if you are not so picky. However, when you do not have a baby, everyone, especially your in-laws, wonders if there is something wrong with you."

The discussion was getting really interesting.

Another single lady chipped in, "well you can adopt or employ the IVF method to have a baby, but you can't adopt a husband, or employ IVF to get one."

The argument kept going back and forth, with everyone trying to defend their stance, as they deemed fit.

I sat there listening, but not contributing, considering the fact that I had a husband and a child, and therefore, didn't think my opinion mattered. I later meditated on the conversation, and realised the ladies who were waiting for either a life partner or a baby defended their arguments based on their unique needs. It was very hard for the single lady to see why a married lady should even dare complain. At least, she has someone to warm her bed at night. The married woman felt the single lady was being very picky with her choices, hence the reason she is still single.

It then occurred to me that no matter what you are waiting for, it could be very hard, especially when there is no end in sight. I don't think one need is superior to the other, but I know it can be challenging waiting for that need to materialise.

It could be waiting in a queue, waiting for the bus, waiting for that job, waiting for financial breakthrough, waiting for your business to boom, waiting for healing, waiting for Mr. Right, waiting for a baby, etc. Whatever the need, it is worth knowing what to do while waiting.

Some tips on waiting on God

1. Focus on God's promises for you. He says to you *"And we know that all things work together for good to those who love God…"* Rom 8:28 (NKJV), *"… I know the plans I have for you…"* Jer 29:11 (NIV), *"… though it tarries…, it will surely come…!"* Hab 2:3 (NKJV), *"Casting all your care upon Him…"* 1 Pet 5:7 (NKJV).

2. Joyce Meyer (I love that woman) said **"Enjoy where you are, on the way to where you are going."** She also said **"Patience is not the ability to wait, but the ability to keep a good attitude while waiting."**

   Waiting isn't easy, but you can choose to have a positive attitude while waiting. Since you already trust God at His word, from the first point stated, you might as well wait joyfully and expectantly, because in the end, it will come to you.

3. Be a source of blessing to others around you. I assure you, you are not the only one waiting for something. You would find this to be true if you just look around. You can be the answer to another person's prayer. By

helping others around you, your problems won't seem so big anymore, and you would actually feel better.

4. Live in the present. Worrying about the future robs you of the present. Worrying cannot change your situation, so enjoy and appreciate God's goodness in your life. Count your blessings. Focus on what you have, not on what you lack.

5. Develop yourself while waiting. Read books, meet people, and develop your gift. This would help you become ready when that job comes, that husband comes, that baby comes, your business grows, or that breakthrough comes.

Sometimes, God might say no to that need. As hard as that might be for you to accept, trust in Him, in the master plan He has for your life, and keep enjoying your life.

It is all working out for your good.

DEO VOLENTE*

While growing up, my mum taught me and my siblings to always attach "By God's grace" as a suffix to our statement, any time we made declarations of a future plan. For example, "I will be travelling tomorrow, by God's grace." Most people who know me know I consciously try to live by this golden rule, because I strongly believe that whatever I do is by God's grace, and not my power.

Now listen, you who say, "Today or tomorrow we will go to this or that city, spend a year there, carry on business and make money." Why, you do not even know what will happen tomorrow. What is your life? You are a mist that appears for a little while and then vanishes. Instead, you ought to say, "If it is the Lord's will, we will live and do this or that." As it is, you boast and brag. All such boasting is evil. Jam 4:13-16 (NIV).

As human beings, we plan, analyse, strategize, and deliberate on our future. However, we must remember our lives are in the hands of God. A lot of people sleep at night, but do not wake up the next morning. What becomes of all their plans? No one can boast of tomorrow, as only God knows what tomorrow holds.

Remember the story of the rich fool who thought he was doing very well, but God told him he would die that night, and not be able to enjoy all he had worked for. The problem was not that the man was rich, but that he believed himself to be invincible, and could enjoy his riches all by himself. Alas, death came knocking.

Start each day by committing it into God's hands. You should, of course, go ahead and make plans, but remember to put God at the centre. As you wake up each day, be thankful for another opportunity to be alive, because it is by the grace of God, and not your doing. The fact that you are alive means your work on earth isn't done yet.

Be a source of blessing to others, and ensure God is directing your every step.

*Deo volente: Latin for "God willing; if nothing prevents it."

WHY WORRY WHEN YOU CAN PRAY?

Why worry, when you can pray?
Trust Jesus, He'll be your stay.
Don't be a doubting Thomas,
Rest fully on His promise,
Why worry, worry, worry, worry when you can pray?
- Alfred B. Smith, John W. Peterson
© 1949 Singspiration Music

I used to sing this song, as a child in Sunday school. It has a very catchy tune, but I never truly understood the meaning till several years later.

For many years, I was addicted to worrying, over-analysing, and trying to figure my way out of situations I didn't like. However, in retrospect, I have now realised that worrying never helped, but trusting God always works.

Time after time, when trials come my way, I always see the same pattern playing out. When I worry, I become frustrated, anxious, panicky, and snappy. To make matters worse, I end up with stomach ache! However, when I trust God, I get peace and breakthrough.

I have countless personal testimonies. When we had childcare issues, God provided help right on time. When our mortgage and bills were due, and we didn't know how we were going to pay for it, God came through for us.

I know worrying might seem easier and more productive than just sitting back, doing nothing and saying "I trust in God." At least with worrying, your mind is busy calculating and analysing, but it all ends in futility.

Glenn Turner describes worry accurately. ***"Worrying is like a rocking chair, it gives you something to do, but gets you nowhere."*** When you worry, all you get is a busy and frustrated mind, but you would not be any closer to the solution. So why worry when you can pray instead. Worrying keeps you focused on the problem, and not God's miraculous power. It could probably be because you don't think God cares enough, or that He is not interested in your issues.

You might have been out of a job for a while, the bills are due for payment, the children's school fees are overdue, the sickness won't leave, or your life just seems to be crumbling before your very eyes. God loves you, and is interested in EVERY single thing that concerns you. He has promised to provide for your needs. He will never leave you nor forsake you.

Think about it. In the dicey situations you have been through in the past, God met your needs, didn't He? So why do you think this situation will be any different? Let go, and trust God. Trust God to meet your needs, and do only what He can do. Once you have done your bit, such as applying for jobs in the case of a lost job, leave the rest to God.

Do you think you can solve your problem much better than God can? When you notice you are trying to figure it all out, it means you do not trust Him.

I love what Joyce Meyer says here. ***"Trusting God often requires not knowing how God is going to accomplish what needs to be done, and not knowing when He will do it."***

He wants us to live by discernment — revelation knowledge, and not head knowledge. This is what is called faith. You need to get to a point in your life that whenever anything you can't handle comes your way, your first response should be "I trust God to take care of this."

God will not give you more than you can bear, so hang in there. He is with you every step of the way, even if you can't feel His presence. You are growing stronger, braver, and more patient through your trials. Though sorrow may last for the night, joy comes in the morning. So stop worrying. Start praying and trusting.

WHAT IS "RIGHT" WITH ME?

Have you ever noticed that you are most likely quick to ask "what is wrong with me?" when things seem to go out of your control, or are not going as planned, or is it just me?

"Why am I not yet married?"
"Why is my husband not like so and so?"
"Why don't I have children?"
"Why are my children not behaving properly?"
"Why is my business not growing?"
"Why don't I have a better-paying job?"
"God, why me?"
"WHAT IS WRONG WITH ME???"

Does it automatically mean when things are not going your way, something is wrong with you? I don't think so, because in life, every mum has her fair share of woes.

Many of us grumble when things don't seem to go our way. Grumbling is certainly not an attractive trait. It will eventually get to a point when your family and friends can't take your moaning and whining anymore. Even God can't stand complainers.

Has it ever occurred to you to ask yourself, "What is right with me?" It might seem like a strange question to ask, but if we start focusing on what is right with us, we might have the right attitude towards life, and not think someone is out to get us, or that we have been cursed.

SO WHAT IS RIGHT WITH YOU?

- **You are alive today**- *some mum somewhere died in her sleep.*
- **You have food to eat**- *so many have nothing to eat.*
- **You have a roof over your head**- *some families have been evicted from their homes.*
- **Your husband sits at home, lazing around, watching football after work**- *some women don't know where their husbands have been for the past two nights.*
- **You can go on holiday when you feel like; you and your husband can travel around**- *those with children need to readjust their plans around school holidays, etc.*
- **Your job pays the bill**s- *some people have been searching for a job since they graduated from school*

I could go on and on, but I believe my point has been made. This is the real world. Bad times are definitely going to come, but don't give up hope. Life isn't fair, as they say, and it owes you nothing. It got here before you!

The good news is that there is light at the end of the tunnel. If only we can change our focus, we would realise this to be true. I know it is easier said than done, but if we want to be appealing to others around us, we must enjoy life, and maintain a good attitude. We need to be thankful to God for the good He has done, and is doing in our lives.

So next time things are not going according to your plan, don't ask yourself "what is wrong with me?" Reframe your mind, ask yourself "what is right with me?" and focus on the good in your life.

Count your blessings, name them one by one,
Count your blessings, see what God hath done!
Count your blessings, name them one by one,
And it will surprise you what the Lord hath done.
- Johnson Oatman, Jr., pub. 1897

APPLYING THE 80-20
RULE TO YOUR LIFE

You have probably heard of the Pareto principle, also known as the 80-20 rule, the law of the vital few, and the principle of factor sparsity.

In the early twentieth century, an Italian economist by the name of Vilfredo Pareto created a mathematical formula describing the unequal distribution of wealth he observed in his country. Pareto observed that approximately 20% of the people controlled or owned 80% of the wealth. In the late 1940s, Dr. Joseph M. Juran, a Quality Management pioneer, attributed the 80-20 Rule to Pareto, calling it Pareto's Principle[1].

This law states that, for many events, approximately 80% of the effects come from 20% of the causes. Ever since then, Pareto's theory of predictable imbalance has since been applied to almost every aspect of life. I have realised that the 80-20 rule can help me focus on what is really important in various aspects of my life.

[1]Source- http://www.pinnicle.com/Articles/Pareto_Principle/pareto_principle.html

Below are some areas where one can apply the 80-20 rule, as a working mum.

PARENTING

A lot of working mums tend to feel guilty because they spend 80% of their time at work, and 20% with their children.

You can choose to look at it this way. When you get to spend time with your children, focus 80% of your energy on the time you get to spend with them. Make it worth their while and yours.

WORK

Approximately 20% of your efforts produce 80% of the results. So find your most productive hours in the day, which isn't usually a lot, protect it, and make the best use of it. During that period, you would achieve a whole lot more than if you work during your less productive hours.

I am more productive in the mornings. By afternoon, my mental effectiveness begins to slow down. Since I have realised this, I use that 20% of my time to focus on my most important tasks, which is 80% of my work. I therefore get more work done during that time.

BUSINESS

Approximately 20% of your consumers would remain loyal to your services or products. It is also a known fact that it is cheaper and easier to retain an existing customer, than to gain new ones. It is therefore wise to invest 80% of your time and resources focusing on those who already buy from you. Focus more on customer retention rather than acquisition. Your existing customers are the ones who would most likely do repeat business with you.

FINANCES

Assign 20% of your monthly income to savings, and 80% to everything else. Make sure that 20% goes into an account you don't readily have access to. How you choose to spend the rest of the 80% is up to you and your value system, but keep the 20% savings intact for the future. Of course, this percentage is not cast in stone. I am simply suggesting 20% as a minimum.

MARRIAGE

In the Tyler Perry's movie, "Why did I get married?", a variant of this law was referred to.

"In love and relationship, you get about 80% of what you need from your mate. Sometimes we meet someone who has that other 20% we are not getting, and the 20% looks real good, but if you trade your 80% for that 20%, then you'll really see how good you had it."

Be thankful for the 80% your spouse is, and let the 20% go.

POSSESSIONS

You use only 20% of what you own 80% of the time. We wear 20% of our favourite clothes and shoes about 80% of the time. Only a small part of what you own is used often. This might help you put things in perspective, and get you to de-clutter the junk in your house. It can also help you rethink buying new items into your home.

FRIENDSHIPS

Only 20% of your friends probably give you 80% of the support, care, and satisfaction you need. 20% of your relationships give 80% of the value. If you thoroughly examine your relationships, you would realise how true this is. You most probably have lot of acquaintances, compared to just a few close friends.

List the people who fall into your 20%, and improve and

nurture those relationships. Invest 80% of your energy and times into those relationships. Those are the people who truly count and matter.

NEEDS/WANTS

When things look bad in your life, you feel like complaining, or are waiting for something, ask yourself this question "Do I want to give up the 80% good in my life because of the 20% I don't have?"

Focus on the 80% that is going on well in your life, and not the 20% that you lack. This will help you to be grateful and positive.

As working mothers, we all have limited resources, be it our time, money, or attention. So to get the most out of our resources, it is important to invest them in only the most profitable areas by applying the 80-20 rule.

WHERE IS YOUR TREASURE?

"Do not lay up for yourselves treasures on earth, where moth and rust destroy and where thieves break in and steal; but lay up for yourselves treasures in heaven, where neither moth nor rust destroys and where thieves do not break in and steal. For where your treasure is, there your heart will be also."
Mat 6:19-21 (NKJV)

A few years ago, when I was living in Nigeria, a lot of investment schemes sprung up, especially the High Yielding Investment Programs (HYIP) such as Nospecto, Seftreg, Wealth Zone, Wealth Solution, Treasure Line, etc. Everywhere I went, I heard people talking about how to make quick and easy money from these schemes.

Everyone I know wants to gain financial freedom. Who wants to be in the rat race forever? Definitely not me! I want to be able to live a very comfortable life, travel round the world, and outsource my cleaning and other chores if possible. My husband and I don't want to depend on our monthly salary to sustain our lifestyle. We want to invest ahead, so that our children can go to the best schools, and have a great life. I am pretty sure many people have similar financial goals.

We all want to be wealthy, rich, and set a legacy for our children, but it seems storing up treasures is all many people are doing. These earthly treasures are fickle, and can disappear in the twinkle of an eye, for whatever reason.

These investment schemes apparently don't last a lifetime. I doubt a good number of them still exist. This is evidence that we cannot depend solely on these schemes or whatever we are storing up as treasures to give us the financial freedom we so desire. So where does that leave us?

One thing I love about God is that He does not leave you stranded. If He tells you what not to do, He definitely will tell you what to do, so there is a way out.

In the scripture above, we are advised to store our treasures in heaven. I believe you are asking, "So how on earth do I store my treasure in heaven?" No pun intended. Well, for starters, you don't have to go up to heaven to store your treasure there. You store your treasure in heaven, here on earth. Getting confused?

What I understand from this scripture is that to store my treasure in heaven, I need to consecrate myself, including my money, fully to God, and use it for His glory. This includes helping people in need.

How many times have people come to meet you to assist them, but you send them away without helping them, even when you are in the position to help? How many of us pay our tithes, donate money to missionaries, orphans, the motherless, prison ministries, non-profit organisations that help those in need, etc.?

These are the opportunities God gives us to store our treasures in heaven. God created us all in His image, so any time you help someone in need, you are doing it for God, and He rewards all good deeds. It may not be apparent because you can't see money increasing in your bank account, but when you invest in other people, God will surely bless you here on earth.

When they say givers never lack, believe it, because it is true. I have experienced this, and heard testimonies of several people who do not necessarily invest their money in stocks and shares, but give and never lack. God always meets their needs.

So dear SWM, invest your money wisely. Lay treasures that cannot be taken away from you. As you invest your money in schemes, stocks, shares, etc., also remember that it is far more rewarding to invest in people and God's work.

Someone's life can be saved today, just because you invested in him or her.

YOU DON'T HAVE TO CATCH THE BALL

When someone throws the ball at you,
you don't have to catch it!

This is a principle I learned a few years ago. Every day, spouses, colleagues, friends, family, etc. throw all kinds of balls at us, and many of us think it is our duty to catch them all. We see ourselves as heroes, and pride ourselves with the ability to rescue our family and friends whenever they are in trouble. However, when we keep doing this, we sometimes begin to feel resentful, blaming others for taking advantage of us, or for not giving us the respect we feel we deserve. It is like a vicious cycle in which we want to please everyone, yet are not happy because we feel manipulated.

Why do we sometimes find ourselves in situations like this? Maybe because we don't want to look bad, we want people to like us, we don't want to let people who depend on us down, or we simply have a rescuer mentality or ego issues.

Other times, it boils down to our inability to say No. Please note that I am not saying we should never be there for our families and friends. What I am saying is that we have a choice to be there for them or not. That way, we won't blame others for taking up all our time, since we made the choice to be available for them in the first place.

The reality is that when we choose not to catch the ball, the owner of the ball will bounce it to someone else, who would eventually catch it. This indicates that you are not the only one in the world who can help. Saying No does not mean you are rejecting the person. It simply means you are rejecting the task or whatever they want you to get involved in.

This is where assertiveness plays a role. I read somewhere that assertiveness is your ability to know who you are, and what you stand for, and then to express these qualities effectively in everyday interactions with people.

Assertiveness is a skill we all have to learn, as it does not come to us naturally. People generally lean towards passiveness (trying to keep peace at all times) or aggression (resorting to ferocity when saying No).

Assertiveness fosters constructive communication and relationship between people. The consequence of being assertive is that people respect your feelings and boundaries. You know you have the right to express your views or beliefs even when it contradicts other people's opinions.

One area where most of us catch the ball even when not necessary is in answering our mobile phones every time it rings. When the phone rings, it suddenly seems like we have to drop everything else. Mobile phones can be a BIG time-stealer. When we pick up the phone, we sometimes end up getting involved in idle chats. We then realise later on that we haven't achieved much, either at work or with house chores.

Sometimes, when I am doing my house chores or working on a task, and my phone rings, I just let it ring out. In fact, I mute the sound of my phone most times. It is my mobile phone, and I can choose to answer it or not. Besides, I can choose to call back. More often than not, if the reason for the call is really important, the caller would either leave a voice mail, or send a text message.

This is not to say I don't appreciate my friends and family, I am anti-social, or I don't want people calling me, but I have learnt that I am in control of my time, and can't catch 'that ball' at that time.

I hope you get the point I am trying to make. Remember that when someone throws the ball at you, you don't have to catch it. You have that choice.

BECOMING ASSERTIVE

Someone once asked me about the difference between being aggressive and being assertive. I must acknowledge that there is a thin line between aggressiveness and assertiveness. However, two key differences when communicating or pushing back is in the tone of your voice, and your body language.

Assertive speaking often involves the use of "I" statements. An example is "I feel upset when you take my book, but don't put it back where you found it." rather than, "You make me feel upset when you take my book, but don't put it back where you found it."

When you are assertive, there is no room for sarcasm or attack.

Below are some tips on how to be assertive.

RECOGNISE THAT PEOPLE ARE DIFFERENT, AND ARE ENTITLED TO THEIR OPINIOINS

People form opinions based on their background, religion,

experiences, values, etc. You should learn to listen to other people's point of view even if you do not agree. There is more than one different position in many situations, so always remain open-minded. By listening to what others have to say, you just might learn something new, and add to your knowledge base. We should also be respectful when expressing our point of views.

LET PEOPLE KNOW WHAT EXACTLY YOU WANT

Wouldn't life have been easier if people could telepathically know what you were thinking, without you having to tell them? I, for one, would find it a relief.

Sometimes, we think if we drop hints, the other person will get the message, but this would most likely lead to assumptions, expectations not being met, and eventually, disappointment. By communicating what exactly you want, you leave no room for guessing games. This gives the other person a chance to respond suitably.

For example, your friend wants you to pick up some items from a shop on your way back from work because it is close to your place of work, but you have a prior engagement you need to attend, and you know going to the shop will delay your meeting. Instead of saying "Okay, I will try to get the items," simply say something like "Aww, I would have loved to help, but unfortunately, that will mean I might run late for my meeting. Can I get them tomorrow, or can someone else help?"

With the latter statement, your friend will not expect you to go to the shop that day. Depending on how urgent she needs it, she would either wait for you to get it the following day, or make other arrangements. Note that you rejected the request, but not the person.

Another example that comes to mind is when you get invited to an event, and you say you will try to attend, knowing fully well that you have no plans to attend. Some people might say it is being diplomatic, but it is simply a lie. I believe it is better to politely decline, stating your reasons, so that way, you not raising the person's expectations. Let your Yes be Yes and, your No be No.

DON'T KEEP QUIET WHEN YOU HAVE STRONG FEELINGS ABOUT AN ISSUE

There are some issues not worth arguing over, and sometimes, the mature thing to do is to keep quiet. Silence, they say, is golden. However, when it comes to your health, safety, core values, or when you know the price of keeping quiet will result into anger or resentment, it is better to speak up than suffer in silence. For example, if your spouse typically stays out late, and this is a behaviour you cannot stand. It is not wise to keep quiet, and frown when he gets home, hoping he gets the message... someday. The appropriate thing to do is speak up in a respectful manner, communicating how you feel about his staying out late to him, so both of you can possibly reach a compromise.

TAKE TIME OUT IF YOU NEED TO CONTAIN YOUR ANGER

Have you noticed that sometimes, you find yourself getting angry during a conversation? At this point, it is better to take a break from the discussion than continuing.

You can hardly communicate effectively when your judgment is clouded with emotions. When you feel much better, you can go back, and present your position more effectively. This is different from cutting others off emotionally, which is a destructive tactic some of us tend to use.

THINK THROUGH YOUR ARGUMENTS BEFORE PRESENTING THEM

Because you sometime think your opinion makes more sense than the other person's, you might get lost in the trivial details that you forget the main points of your arguments. If you want to effectively get your point across, think through the issues, and drill down to the important points. The other person might be much more willing to listen if your ideas are presented in an organised and consistent manner.

So these are just a few examples on how to be assertive. It is definitely a useful life skill one has to practice from time to time.

MAXIMISING YOUR MORNINGS

A lot of working mothers struggle with waking up early. If this is an issue for you, I want to teach you how to stop this habit, and get you to start maximising your mornings.

Why should you wake up early? Because mornings are such a great time to connect with God, and get a lot done before various distractions takes over. Another reason is because you are setting up a prosperous future for yourself.

Tom Corley, on his website, RichHabitsInstitute.com, summarises a few of the differences between the habits of the rich and the poor. One of these is that 44% of wealthy wake up three hours before work starts vs. 3% of poor.

From as far as memory serves me, I have always LOVED my sleep, and I did not let anything interfere with my sleep time. I think I can safely say I was a sleep addict! It was so bad that I would snooze my alarm at 6:30 a.m., and finally get out of bed at 7:00 a.m. I would then have just one hour to get ready for work! This resulted in me always having hurried mornings.

The flaw with daily routine was that because I started my day wrong, my whole day was usually messed up. I never had time to connect with God, and I was always on rush mode. Weekends were no better; I slept late, and woke up late. Another productive day wasted!

I was constantly on the edge, and stressed out. Twenty four hours were never enough, and I didn't seem to know what to do about it. I knew I had to make a change, but didn't know where to start. I even asked God to wake me up early, which He did, but I still couldn't get out of bed. I did not find a solution until I put a conscious plan of action in place.

Now, I get up around 5:30 a.m., and I get to maximise my mornings before my family gets up. I can hardly believe how productive I now am, as a result of simply choosing to wake up early. I am so glad my days of sleep addiction are over!

So how did I do it? It was actually easier than I thought.

DEFINE THE PURPOSE

What do you need to accomplish by waking up early, of what benefit is it to you? You need a big WHY to wake up early, if not, there will be no point in getting up early.

For me, the main reason I wanted to wake up early was so I could

- spend time with God
- start my day in a relaxed and unhurried state
- exercise sometimes
- write
- plan the rest of the day

… with NO INTERFERENCE from anybody.

Have you ever tried to work out or write, with a toddler getting in between your legs and pressing your keyboard? It is not a funny experience.

I have realised that the early hours of the morning are so peaceful and quiet for me. I am usually alert and productive, compared to evenings.

INFORM YOUR FAMILY AHEAD

Let your spouse and children know there are going to be some changes at home.

Make them aware of the fact that mummy will have her alone time. If your little ones get out of bed early, send them back to bed, or get them engaged in something else. If you still have a baby, get your husband on baby duty time, if possible. They will have your attention at other times of the day, so it is only a fair price to pay.

PLAN YOUR MORNING ON THE PREVIOUS NIGHT

Map out how long each of your activity will take. For example, my outline is something like this:

5:20 a.m.: Get out of bed

5:25 a.m.: Get a cup of water or green tea

5:30 a.m. to 6:00 a.m.: Read my bible, worship, and pray

6:00 a.m. to 7:00 a.m.: Write my book, and plan the rest of my day

7:00 a.m. to 7:20 a.m.: Work out with my exercise DVD, if possible

7:25 a.m.: Day starts with family

This outline evolves, depending on my current situation.

I suggest you write out your plan too, and mentally tell yourself before you go to bed, "I will wake up at 5:30 a.m. (or any time that works for you), and get out of bed." This will help you put your mind on alert. Once your mind is on board, your body will follow suit.

SLEEP EARLY!

It is only logical that if you want to wake up early, you should sleep early. As it is commonly said, "Early to bed, early to rise." It is recommended that an adult should have six to seven hours of sleep every day, so calculate the hours, and go to bed depending on the time you need to start your day.

The good news is that by the time you start waking up early, your body will adjust, and you'll find that you start to feel sleepy earlier than before.

UTILISE THE PREVIOUS NIGHT

Get everything you need for the next morning ready at night. Decide what clothes and shoes you and the children will wear. This ensures that as soon as you wake up, you would not be wasting time looking for your materials. You would already be equipped to start the day right!

EAT A LIGHT MEAL FOR DINNER

Eat a light meal before 7.00 p.m. Your food will digest faster, and this will help you sleep better at night, thereby making it easier for you to get out of bed early.

IN THE MORNING

Actually get out of bed

This is the hardest step. Once your alarm goes off, open your eyes, sit up, and then get out of bed. Make sure you don't close your eyes, and don't get back into bed. I have to emphasise on not getting back into bed because you WILL be tempted to get back into bed for a few seconds. Don't give in!

Gather your materials, and walk out of the room. Drink some water. Amongst other benefits, drinking water helps you stay hydrated, and boosts your metabolism. Once you walk out of your room, you are home-free.

Find a quiet spot in the house

It should be preferably not your bedroom. I choose the dining room to have my quiet time, and do my writing. When you find your spot, start doing the things you outlined in your plan.

Exercise

If you use a DVD to work out, get it done. If you jog or run outside, get going. If you currently do not exercise, consider starting. Exercising is beneficial in so many ways. It energises you, and keeps you fit.

Get support

Some people are habitual early birds, such as my friend who wakes up at 5.00 a.m. unfailingly every day. You can get the support of someone who is an early bird, to check up on you from time to time.

Alternatively, if you have a friend who also wants to start waking up early, you can encourage and be accountable to each other. Maybe you could even take turns waking each other up!

YOU CAN DO IT TOO!

If Aloted, the queen of sleep, could do it, so can you. Set your own pace, find and do what works for you, based on your current situation. Whatever the case, remember the goal is to GET OUT OF BED EARLY.

Sometimes you might slip, maybe due to illness or circumstances beyond your control. Don't beat yourself up about it. Just make sure you don't go back to your old habits.

Take it one day at a time. This doesn't mean you can't indulge yourself once in a while, with sleeping in. However, once you start this new journey, it would be more of a treat, than the norm for you.

I still love sleeping, but my desire to accomplish my goals, and become a Super Working Mum has now surpassed my desire to sleep. This is what gets me up at 5.30 a.m. in the morning.

Are your desires in life strong enough to hurl you out of bed, and into action?

THE ART OF KINDNESS

If only we were kinder to one another, the world would be a better place to live in. You need to be kind to your spouse, children, friends, enemies, strangers, etc. You need to be kind to yourself.

WHAT DOES IT MEAN TO BE KIND?

Kindness is love in action. In practical terms, kindness means different things to each one of us, but here are some basic acts of kindness.

Kindness means:
- doing unto others, as you want them to do to you
- being supportive of others
- speaking words of encouragement, and soothing words, rather than harsh words
- helping out a friend in need, even if it is inconvenient
- listening when a friend needs to vent
- being sensitive to the needs of our spouses, children, friends, etc.
- telling the truth in LOVE, not what others want to hear,

but what they need to hear
- · being committed to those you care about
- · helping strangers when they need assistance

What does kindness mean to you? How can you perfect the art of kindness? Below listed are examples of ways you can display the art of kindness in your everyday life.

1. Take a minute to direct a stranger who is lost, even when you are in a hurry
2. Say thank you to the bus or cab driver
3. Write an email to your team members, telling them what great job they are doing
4. Pay your spouse a compliment
5. Ask your children how their day went, and really listen to their response
6. Offer to babysit for a single mum
7. Give someone an interesting book you have just finished reading
8. Visit and take some cooked food to a friend who just put to bed
9. Write an encouraging note to a friend who is discouraged
10. Send your clients cards on their birthdays

Ask God to give you opportunities to show kindness to at least one person every day, and when that opportunity comes, just go on and be kind. Your life will be better for it. Also, your simple act of kindness can make all the difference in that someone's life.

It is an interesting fact of history that the Romans confused the Greek word 'Christos' (Christ) with the word 'Chrestos,' (kind). [2]See how many people you can confuse each day.

[2]http://www.mountainman.com.au/essenes/chrestos%20christos.htm

SELF-CARE 101

One of the ways we can live fulfilled lives is by taking good care of ourselves. This is something a lot of women, especially mums, find difficult to do because we have being subconsciously taught that when you have a family, you should not think about yourself anymore. Your husband and children come first, they say.

Also, society tends to make women feel their needs are no longer important or valid once they have a family. They make you feel you can't have fun anymore because you are now a mother.

We all know that being a working mum is hard. You may feel like you live on a rollercoaster, or that your life is being pulled in several directions, with your work tugging at you on one end, and your husband, kids, and other commitments on the other. However, crumpling into a pile of exhaustion and guilt isn't the answer. Instead, tell yourself "this is my life, and I'm going to make it work for me, by taking care of myself, by God's grace."

I am telling you it is okay to take care of yourself. It is not just okay, it is IMPORTANT you take care of YOU, because until you take care of You, you cannot really take care of others.

Successful working mums have learnt that when they don't make time for themselves, they wouldn't be as effective and happy as they ought to. And we all know an unhappy mum makes an unhappy home.

So how can you incorporate some self-care into your life?

CONNECT WITH GOD IN PRAYER AND MEDITATION

Your first step to caring for yourself spiritually, emotionally, and mentally is by connecting with your heavenly father throughout the day. Our source of strength is God, so we need to draw strength from Him every day, by spending time with Him.

He fills you with power, strength, and energy, and refuels you on a daily basis. He adds the Super to your Natural. It is therefore imperative that you stay plugged in to Him, so you can accomplish all you need to, through His supernatural strength.

TAKE CARE OF YOUR HEALTH

Do regular medical check-ups with your doctor. Eat energy-boosting foods such as oranges, bananas, almonds, oats, broccoli, spinach, and green smoothies. Eliminate junk food from your diet, exercise regularly, and take multivitamins. Drink lots of water. Water is very good for you.

Health is wealth. Without good health, you cannot enjoy your life, family, and work, so take care of your health.

FORGIVE AND LET THINGS GO

Learn to forgive yourself and others. Harbouring bitterness and resentment does nothing good for you. It would only harm you, and can have a negative impact on your health. When we forgive others, it is not usually for their benefit, but ours. You set yourself free when you forgive.

Studies have shown that unforgiveness and bitterness can be the root cause of deadly sicknesses such as heart attacks, high blood pressure, headaches, and chronic pain. Holding on to anger can affect your emotional and physical health. The knowledge of this is enough reason for you to forgive others.

You should also learn not to be too sensitive. When people say things that offend you, learn to shake it off. If you find it hard to forgive others, or even yourself, ask God to help you. He will.

SLEEP

Studies have shown that sleep-deprivation can cause you to gain weight. I know many mums are on a mission to lose weight, so let this motivate you to sleep some more!

Health experts say we need a minimum of six to seven hours of sleep every night. By getting a good night rest, you would wake up more refreshed, and be ready to start your day, energised. Take power naps at work, if you can.

Right after delivery, you may find it difficult to sleep sometimes, especially if your baby wakes up at night to feed, so try to get some sleep during the day. Sleep when your baby is sleeping. The dishes and laundry can wait. Life is too short to be folding laundry. Better still, you can outsource the chores.

If you are anxious about something, and can't sleep, commit it into God's hands, and go to bed! Your staying up late at night is not going to solve the issue, so why not leave it to the one who neither slumbers nor sleeps, and get yourself a good night rest?

DETOX YOUR FRIENDS

Stay around only those who motivate you to be your best. It is important for your self-care that you stay around positive people.

Late Jim Rohn, a self-help guru said *"You are the average of the five people you spend the most time with."* Carry out an assessment of your immediate circle. If the friends you keep are not changing your life for the better, if they are infecting you instead of you affecting them, it is time to let them go. Get rid of all toxic relationships in your life.

Get a mentor, hang out with people that will inspire you to be your best, and make sure you are a blessing to the people in your life.

SCHEDULE YOUR SELF-CARE HOURS

Schedule a regular relaxation activity for yourself, and protect that appointment as if it is the most important agenda on your schedule. It probably isn't, but unless you treat it as such, it will get dropped off the minute something seemingly more important comes up.

Once your family knows about your designated self-care time, they will learn to respect that time, and let you be, but you have to make it clear to them from the onset.

Get a massage, manicure, or pedicure. Take a walk, go to the cinema alone, read a book, or do something just for you. Have a list of different activities you can engage yourself in, and choose randomly from them. If you don't make time for it, it won't happen. If something else urgent comes up, and you can't make your appointment, reschedule it, and don't just let it slide.

If this is an uncharted course for you, and you are terrified of leaving your child with a sitter or your husband, you can take baby steps. Try to take a 30-minute walk, and when you begin to feel more comfortable, increase the duration and activities.

Remember the things you used to enjoy before you became a mum. They could be reading, writing, singing, knitting, painting, gardening, sewing, or designing. Rekindle your passion for such recreational activities.

You may begin to wonder "but what of all these other things I need to do? I can't just up and go, I need to be here for everyone." Dear mum, you need to learn to delegate more. Think about it, if you keep doing everything for your children, how are they ever going to learn to do things by themselves? See it as you empowering them for the future, and helping them become responsible adults. Most importantly, this puts less pressure on you to get things done for everyone.

Involve your husband. Some women tend to think their husbands can't do anything right, and would therefore, rather not involve them in home affairs. Even though they may not take care of the children the way you do, they will most likely have their own method, so give them the opportunity to display their way of doing things.

You could also employ a babysitter or cleaner to help with house chores. There is no rule that states that mummy should do everything.

GO ON A RETREAT

While I was growing up, my mum regularly went on weekend retreats. In hindsight, I believe this probably helped her become a better mum because she deliberately took time away from her everyday life, to recharge spiritually, mentally, and emotionally.

A retreat is the withdrawal to a safe quiet place for those seeking solitude, relaxation, rejuvenation, healing, uplifting fellowship, or spiritual contemplation.

You may think it is impossible to just up and go away for the weekend, but your family will thank you for it, because you will be a better person, wife, and mum when you take out time for yourself.

CEOs of organisations take regular retreats in order to

strategise on how to make their companies better. You are the CEO of your home, so if you want to run your home successfully, be a better wife and mum, you need to take out time for yourself.

Begin to apply these self-care tips, and see the huge difference it will make in your life.

TAKE TIME TO REST

I know resting doesn't come naturally to some women, especially mothers, but I advise you to develop the habit of resting. You were designed to work for some time, and get some rest later.

I once read somewhere that the body was meant to rejuvenate twice a day. One short sleep session during the day, and one long sleep session at night, for about six to seven hours.

If you keep working without resting, you will eventually break down, and be of no use to anyone. Even God, who doesn't sleep nor slumber, rested for one day, after creating the world in six days. Let us therefore, take a cue from our Heavenly Father, and learn to rest. Resting is part of God's plan for your life.

I know it sounds counterintuitive, but by taking one day to rest, you will be more productive during the other six days of the week. You will feel rejuvenated physically, mentally, emotionally, and spiritually. You will be in a much better, happier, calmer, and less stressed position to serve your family when you rest.

Resting doesn't necessarily mean lying down, and not doing anything. If you are tired, you can get some sleep. Your rest time could also be spent doing what you enjoy doing apart from regular office work or household chores. Resting could mean spending time with friends, reading, or taking part in recreational activities you enjoy. Shut work down, take that overdue vacation, enjoy life, relax, and fall in love with having good fun.

So to you lovely super working mama reading this, no matter how busy you are, you need to take time to rest. Just as I mentioned earlier, it might not come easily or naturally, but you can do it. When you take time to rest, you will also be teaching your children that it is okay to relax. The world will not fall apart if you do.

Everyone and everything can wait while you rest.

GOOD HEALTH AND WELLNESS

What is the state of your health? Are you constantly feeling tired, worn out, and overwhelmed? This probably means you are taking on more than you can, not eating right, exercising, and resting.

Some mums feel guilty about taking time out for themselves, but you shouldn't. You can choose to see it from this perspective, if you do not take care of yourself, how would you be able to take care of your family and other important things? If you burn and crash, what is the good in that?

We as mums need to prioritise caring for ourselves. This is not a selfish thing, but a wise thing to do! By taking care of your health and wellbeing, you are taking care of your family.

EAT HEALTHY

To maintain a good health, you need to be intentional about what you put into your body. Remember garbage in, garbage out.

- Swap high calorie or high fat processed foods with

more natural whole foods

- Substitute refined grained foods with whole grain foods.
- Boil, roast, or stir fry instead of deep-frying
- Bulk up meals with vegetables (carrots, broccoli, cauliflower, green peas, etc.) and protein (fish, chicken)
- Eat all three meals
- Snack on fruits or green smoothies instead of junk food

I know a lot of mothers, including me, sometimes skip breakfast because they are busy and rushing, but remember that breakfast is the most important meal of the day. So plan your day in such a way that you can have some breakfast. Make sure you eat a healthy breakfast, which can include wholegrain cereals and fibre, to keep you energised throughout the day.

KEEP FIT

Exercise is a great way to maintain good health and wellness. Register with a gym, or get an exercise DVD for home workout sessions. I know some mums use Jillian Michaels ripped in 30 days or the intensity workout DVD, but I use the Zumba DVD on my Wii, because I like dancing, and love to incorporate some fun into my workout sessions. Choose what works for you.

If you can't dedicate time to exercise, you can be creative during the day:

- Take walks during your lunch break
- If you use the bus, alight a few stops before your intended destination, and trek the remaining part of the journey
- If you can swim, go swimming with the family
- Ditch the car, and walk if your destination isn't far

CARE FOR YOURSELF

Doing things you love is also important for your health, sanity, and wellbeing. When was the last time you sat down to read a novel, or just enjoy a few minutes of peace and quiet? Be intentional about taking care of yourself, by scheduling ME time into your busy schedule. If you don't schedule it, it won't happen.

God's will for you is to be healthy and well, but it is up to you to make it happen. Maintaining a healthy lifestyle on a busy schedule will definitely require dedication, proactivity, and good time management on your part, but it is doable.

THE POWER IN DELEGATING

Every SWM must know how to delegate. Delegating gives you more time to focus on doing what you love. It gives you time to channel your energy into your core functions such as being a wife and mum.

There is no sense in doing everything by yourself when you can delegate. You will not get any medals for working yourself to the ground when you can ask for help or delegate instead. You need to know how to work smart rather than working hard.

Your life would become easier when you share the burden of household chores and business tasks. How would it look if the CEO of McDonalds was downstairs flipping burgers and taking orders? Strange, right? It goes same way for you. You, as the CEO of your home, should be 'upstairs', making strategic decisions, and project-managing, not doing all the work.

DELEGATING AT HOME

Some mums seem to love the fact that their family is

dependent on them, but dependence on you doesn't serve you or your family well. If you fall sick, it will be more stressful for everyone in your family to make adjustments, because they are not used to functioning without you!

You probably feel you do things better, faster and, more efficiently than other people in your family, but if you keep doing everything by yourself, you would not be teaching your children how to be responsible. Children need to know they have duties, as part of the family, and mummy isn't their servant.

Assign age-appropriate tasks to your children, and get your husband involved in helping out as well. Lower your expectations, and with practice, your family will become better at doing their tasks.

If you can afford a cleaner, get one! In the UK, where I live, you can hire a cleaner for three hours for £30 or slightly less. I believe three hours of your time is a lot more than £30, so it only makes sense to outsource some chores to experts in their field, so you could use that time for something else. Take a cue from the proverbs 31 woman. She didn't do it all by herself, she got help.

What are you doing for your children that they can do for

themselves? What tasks can you delegate today so that you can have more time to spend with your family or yourself?

Some mums pay their children to do chores, but I do not think it is a good practice. I think by paying your children to do chores, you are making them believe they have to be financially rewarded for everything. My children are part of the family, and should contribute their quota to the growth and maintenance of the family.

DELEGATING AT WORK

In the Bible, when Moses was attending to the drama of the children of Israel, Jethro, his father-in-law, called him aside, and told him he would burn out if he continued that way. He advised him to delegate to other God-fearing men, and only deal with difficult cases. Moses was wise to take his father-in-law's advice, and I believe he was less-burdened after delegating.

Are you a micromanager at work? To be effective in your role, you need to delegate tasks to your subordinates. Not only will you be empowering them to do better, you will also make life easier for yourself, and be more efficient. Initially, it may seem slow and long-winded, but once there are processes in place, you will have a shorter turnaround time.

Are you in business? Delegate the tasks you do not enjoy, or your non-core tasks to a virtual assistant. Your business will grow faster since you will be concentrating on the core tasks that will move your business forward.

I know finances could be the biggest factor stopping you from outsourcing. You can start small. There are lots of website where you can hire a virtual assistant at affordable rates, such as fiverr.com and odesk.com.

The wisdom in not trying to conquer the whole world by yourself is what makes you super.

A FUN-FILLED AND
FULFILLING MARRIAGE

Before you became a mother, you were a wife. Your next priority after God should be your spouse, not your children. Many mums get it mixed up sometimes, by focusing more on their children, at the expense of their marriage.

The state of your marriage will have an impact on your children. What is the current state of your marriage? Are you in a healthy and loving relationship with your husband?

Your children need to see that you and your husband love, and are in love with each other. They need to see you are always united. This doesn't mean you can't argue in front of your children. In fact, contrary to popular opinion, I think couples should argue and resolve some arguments in the presence of their children. This will let them understand that life isn't all about roses and fairy tales, and will teach them how to resolve conflict, as they grow older.

Commit to loving your spouse and growing together, not apart. When your children leave home, you will be left alone with your spouse, so start nurturing and investing in your marital relationship now.

As Christians, marriage is meant to be forever, so you might as well enjoy it! Here are some ways to maintain a fun and fulfilled marriage, which I am also working on:

UNDERSTAND YOUR HUSBAND

By recognising what your husband likes and dislikes, and other little, yet important details, you can avoid a lot of conflict.

GO ON REGULAR DATES

Have a date night you are both committed to. Come up with various activities you can both engage in together. Get a babysitter to watch the children if you can afford one, or swap babysitting days with a close friend. Use date nights to enjoy each other's company.

SHOW AFFECTION

Find opportunities to show affection to your spouse. Write him notes he can find and read in his office. Send him text messages to let him know you are thinking about him. Hug him as much as you can.

PRAY TOGETHER

It is commonly said that a family that prays together stays together. If you are not opportune to pray together, or you are married to an unbeliever, you can pray for him. Pray for your marriage. God is listening, and will answer.

WEATHER THE STORMS TOGETHER

When trials and tribulations come, don't argue with each other. Remain calm, stand together, and encourage each other. Tell yourselves "this too shall pass."

ADJUST YOUR EXPECTATIONS

Don't burden your spouse with the role of being your saviour. You will only get disappointed. Just like you, your husband is human, not perfect, and will make mistakes. Instead, cast your burdens on God, and trust Him to completely meet all your needs.

LISTEN AND COMMUNICATE

Listen to your husband wholeheartedly when he is talking to you. Give him your full attention. Echo his words back to him, so you are both clear you understand what he is saying. This will let him know that you respect and value what he has to say. You should also not assume your husband can read your mind, especially when you need help around the home. Speak up when something isn't working for you in your marriage.

STAY UNITED

Stay united, especially when it comes to making decisions about your children. A lot of children play their parents against each other, in order to get their way. Even if you don't agree, wait till you are alone to voice your objections. United you stand, divided you fall!

SPICE THINGS UP IN THE BEDROOM

Don't let tiredness or children get in the way. Schedule sex into your routine, if you have to. If you need help in the love-making department, ask God to help. He invented sex after all!

Throughout the Bible, God uses marriage to depict his desired relationship with humankind. The devil is totally against this. He knows God designed the institute of marriage, and the family institution brings God joy. He is therefore out to destroy marriages.

If you and your spouse have drifted apart, ask God to restore the love you once had for each other. Nothing is impossible for God to do. He can restore what the devil has stolen, if you let Him. It may require counselling, or sacrifice on both parts.

Finally, take up this daily challenge to improve the state of your marriage. Replace busyness, jealousy, and pettiness with hugs, kisses, and kindness. The more you give in your marriage, the more you get in return.

PARENTING INTENTIONALLY

Parenting intentionally involves teaching and training our children in the way of the Lord. We might read the Bible to our children, take them to church, sing Christian songs, but the best way we can train our children in the way of the Lord is by the way we live our lives.

Our children observe us, how we respond to challenges, relate to our spouses, handle money, and the words we speak. They watch everything we do, and take their cue from us. We are the light that illuminates the path our children take.

I used to think my daughter picked up her cheeky behaviour from friends at school, till the Holy Spirit told me to look closer to home. Half of the time, she was picking it up from me! Now I make a conscious effort to behave appropriately, asking God to help me be a better person, so I can model an exemplary life to my children.

My parents for both lived godly lives at home, and outside of the home, and I am grateful to them for that.

Here are a few characteristics of Intentional Parents.

They:

- train, teach, and instruct their children in the way of the Lord
- pray for and with their children daily
- teach them, from an early age, how to relate with their heavenly father
- encourage interdependency in their children. They allow their children to learn the life lessons they need. They allow them make their own mistakes
- adjust their expectations to the age and reasoning capacity of their children They don't overreact when their children fall short of their expectations
- discipline their children even when it is inconvenient, infuriates their children, or makes them look bad as parents. They realise they are parents, not friends!
- encourage and praise their children when they do the right thing. They know this will help their children succeed

How can you become intentional in your parenting today? Ask God to help you commit to being an intentional parent from this moment.

"MONKEY SEE, MONKEY DO"

You probably know what the expression "monkey see, monkey do" means. It is usually used as an analogy for children imitating what they see adults do, without necessarily asking why.

You may have noticed that your children do what they see you do, rather than what you tell them to do. They take their cue from you. Below are simple ways we can influence our children's attitudes.

- If you want them to be confident, be confident
- If you want them to be truthful, speak the truth
- If you want them to have a thankful attitude, be thankful
- If you want them to be courteous and kind, show courtesy to others
- If you want them to be prayerful, let them see you pray
- If you want them to save money, start saving
- If you want them to be content, stop grumbling
- If you want them to watch less TV, reduce your TV-watching time

- If you want them to read books, read some yourself
- If you want them to eat healthy, stay away from junk food

What improvements do you want to see in your child? Examine yourself to be sure you are displaying those traits. If not, aim to work on them. You are the primary example in your child's life.

BE PROFESSIONAL

Professionalism means you are committed to a certain standard of conduct, regardless of the circumstances. Just because we are mothers, overwhelmed, or tired as a result of the various roles we play does not give us the liberty to act as we wish at work. In fact, one of your policies should be that, to the best of your abilities, your home affairs will not interfere with your work, and vice versa.

Perception is key, and if you are not perceived to be professional in the work place, there is a limit to the level you can rise to in your profession, even if you are the smartest or most intelligent person at work.

I once had a colleague who was very smart. However, because she was always late to work and client meetings, during her appraisal, the partners and managers didn't think she was qualified for a promotion. Because they doubted her dependability, they doubted her professionalism. She had been praying for a promotion, and probably blamed God for not getting it, but in reality, she had only herself to blame.

Ask yourself, "How do I currently conduct myself at work? Do I give glory to God with the way I conduct myself? What goes through my colleagues' minds when they hear my name?"

If you don't think your conduct is Christ-like, ask God to help you make a change.

SIX WAYS TO BE PROFESSIONAL AT WORK

Get to work and meetings early

Your name shouldn't be associated with that of the latecomers. Your aim should be to get to work at least five to ten minutes before the official starting hour. That way, you would be well-settled before you begin to work. Constantly strolling in late doesn't portray good work ethics.

An attitude of punctuality will also vindicate you on rare occasions when you cannot avoid being late, maybe due to traffic or an emergency. You would have already built a good reputation at this point.

If you work for yourself, make sure you arrive at client or networking meetings on time.

Dress professionally

The first thing your clients and colleagues notice about you is your appearance. You need to leave a good impression always. Remember that the way you dress is the way you will be addressed. You don't have to break a bank to look professional. Wear clothes that are well-pressed, fit for your size, and smart-looking. Anything revealing should be left at home, for the eyes of your husband only.

Find out your company's policy on dressing if you don't already know it, then invest in quality attires for work. Even if you work from home, have outfits you can wear to client meetings.

Deal with family and home emergencies professionally
If you have an emergency at home, inform your superiors and colleagues immediately. If you have to work from home, be reachable on your phone or via email. Don't go AWOL; keep the lines of communication open as much as you can.

If the situation is really serious, and demands your full attention, you can take time off work, as your productivity may suffer if you try to combine work and an emergency.

If you are working with clients, but running behind schedule, keep them in the loop of the emergency, and don't go quiet on them. Most clients don't mind getting their work after a deadline, if something beyond your control comes up. What they might mind is not hearing from you for days.

Have integrity

Let your Yes be Yes, and your No be No. If you say you are going to call a client at a particular time, do so. If you say you are going to finish your assigned tasks on a team project on a particular date, endeavour to do so. If for some reasons, you can't finish it, communicate this to the other parties involved. Be seen as an honest and dependable person at work.

Being honest may not be a popular choice, especially at work, but that is what we have been called to do, as people of integrity.

Use social media wisely

If you are having a bad day at work, or your boss is frustrating you, Facebook or Twitter is NOT the place to rant. Pray about it, call a friend if you need to whine, or write it on paper to release any tension in you, and tear it up thereafter. Don't, I repeat, don't rant on social media. It will most likely come back to bite you. Once it gets out there, you can never take it back.

Be calm

It is almost inevitable that conflict will arise with colleagues or clients. You will meet rude and obnoxious people at work. If someone disrespects you or picks on you, make an intentional effort not to lose your temper. Walk away if you can, and ask God to give you the patience to deal with the situation appropriately.

Which one of these six tips do you need to work on? Ask for the help of the Holy Spirit, as we cannot do anything without Him.

Being professional is about treating others the way you love to be treated. It is about doing your best, and being diligent in your work. It is about bringing glory to God through your life.

SLEEPING ON DUTY

Do you sometimes find it difficult to stay awake at work? Do you find yourself sleeping on duty occasionally?

Dozing or even getting caught dozing at work can be embarrassing and unprofessional in the workplace. To avoid this happening, let's explore practical ways to help you stay awake at work.

FIND THE ROOT CAUSE

First of all, you need to determine the cause of your tiredness. Lack of adequate night sleep may cause your body to try catching up with sleep during the day. If you can deal with the root cause, then half of your problem is solved.

A few reasons we find ourselves not being able to stay awake at work could be

- Poor sleeping pattern, maybe because your child wakes you up at night
- Staying up late to catch up on your chores or a TV program

- Unhealthy diet or eating late
- Illness or poor health
- Stress

There was a time I used to be very lethargic and sleepy at work, only to be later diagnosed with low blood pressure. I was asked by my physician to increase my salt intake, and that solved the problem. My point is, investigate the reason behind your sleepiness at work, and deal with it.

I am aware that sometimes, even getting six or seven hours of sleep might not stop you from nodding off during your work hours. One or more of the tips below should work for you.

1. **Chew gum**- chewing gum gets your mouth moving up and down. This could help you stay awake at work.
2. **Snack on fruits**- eating apples and grapes are healthy and excellent ways to release energy into your system, and help you stay alert.
3. **Take a walk**- use this opportunity to walk to the water dispenser for a quick drink, or stop by at a colleague's desk to say hi or find out how their day is going, but take care not to chat for too long.
4. **Splash cold water** on your face and neck. Cold water should jolt you from your slumber.
5. **Drink coffee or caffeinated tea**- I personally don't

drink coffee, as it gets me agitated, but some people swear by it. I recommend you limit the amount of coffee or caffeinated tea you drink, in order to avoid counterproductive effects.

6. Instead of coffee or energy drink, I prefer to **drink green tea.** Though it also has caffeine, its small dose is just enough to give you a boost, but doesn't induce the jittery and anxious feelings typically associated with other caffeinated beverages.

7. **Take a walk right after lunch**- doing this prevents your food from sitting in your stomach, and not digesting on time. You get to stretch, and also bask in some fresh air and sunlight, if any. Also, **avoid eating a large lunch**- this can weigh you down, and lead to lethargy and sleepiness.

8. I haven't tried this before, but I read somewhere that **inhaling essential oils** such as rosemary or peppermint oil for a few seconds can help you stay awake. I would definitely try this out sometime soon.

9. My last and tried method is taking a **10 to 15 minutes power nap** in your car or the rest room. This should set you straight. Just make sure you don't have any meetings or deadlines during that period. Don't disappear for long!

If none of the above works, it might simply mean you find your work boring or monotonous, and that is a different problem entirely.

It is usually better to deal with the reason behind poor sleeping habits than trying to fight off sleep at work. However, the above tips should work if you use them.

BUILD STRONG AND
MEANINGFUL FRIENDSHIPS

Building and investing in solid relationships with other women with values similar to yours will propel you to lead a successful life. No (wo)man is an island. We were made to interact with others, be of support, and encourage one another.

We all have our bad days, when we feel inadequate, or days when we feel like we are not doing well at anything. Having a support system makes you realise you are not the only one going through challenges. Your friends can help you through difficult times, by reassuring you, and praying for you.

To make a friend, you must first be a friend. Go out of your way to encourage another mum. Extend a helping hand. Be genuinely interested in that person's life. Ask questions, and take time to listen. Also, share few details about yourself so that you can earn trust. This is how strong friendships are formed and fostered.

I once read this somewhere, and it stuck with me ever since. "In any relationship you are in, aim to be the bigger giver." Give of your time, resources, skills, support, money, and encouragement, without expecting anything in return. When you give, it will come back to you.

Let your words ALWAYS be tools to uplift, influence, inspire, and encourage others. If your words are not going to help others, it is better not to say anything, because once you say something, you can't take it back.

Late Jim Rohn, in the law of averages, stated that you are the average of the five people you spend the most time with. Whose company are you keeping? Be intentional about the people you hang out with. Evil communication corrupts good manners. Stay away from negative people, who are always critical or spiteful, whose words do not match their actions, or who want to put you down. You can support them, but they shouldn't be your best buddies.

If the people around you are infecting you, instead of you affecting them, it is time to change your company.

Conflicts will occur in your relationships, and some might get messy sooner or later. This is not necessarily a bad thing. Try to resolve conflicts quickly when they occur, by listening to the other person's perspective, putting yourself in the other person's shoes, accepting your wrong, respectfully stating how you feel, and forgiving any offence.

As we get older and go through different phases of life such as marriage, parenthood, changing jobs, starting a business, etc., what we want or need out of our friendships may change. Even though old connections may be a source of comfort and security, they may no longer be beneficial to both parties.

Take the time to assess whether you really enjoy spending time with some of your old friends. If you don't, begin to limit the energy you put into those friendships, and invest that time in getting to know new people.

Also, some of your old friends may also start to spend less time with you. Be intuitive when this is happening, and don't feel bad about it. They also have a choice to decide who they want to spend their time with.

Building strong and meaningful friendship is hard work, and takes time to develop, but when you find the right friends who truly care about you, it will be worth it.

LIFE LESSONS FROM A CRAWLING BABY

It is amazing how much you can learn about life, just by watching a crawling baby. Professor J, my son, started to roll on the ground when he was six months old. I remembered my dad telling me that as a child, I never crawled, but rolled from one side of the room to the other, so I assumed Professor J was going to do the same.

Then one day, I noticed he was not rolling anymore. Instead, he was dragging himself on his belly. I found it very fascinating. Soon after, it was not just his belly, but his elbows and knees. He was very fast and good with it. It looked like he was swimming.

By the time I completed the first draft of this book, he had started crawling on all fours. Although sometimes, he still prefers to drag himself around on his belly. It is intriguing to watch him learn more about himself and his environment.

WHAT HAVE I LEARNED FROM THIS VERY SIMPLE ACT?

Crawling is a personal experience

I know experts say a baby should crawl on all fours, but as long as a child can get to point A to B, it doesn't really matter the method he employs. So is our life's journey. People and society tell you there is a certain way to be successful and make it in life. As long as you are doing what God has called you to do, you don't have to follow a 5-point checklist to succeed. You are on the right path, and it doesn't matter what everyone else is saying or doing.

Be Persistent

Babies are definitely the best teachers of persistence. Have you seen a baby trying to crawl or walk? He isn't scared to try. If he fails the first time, he does not give up, but tries again. He may seem unsure of what he is doing, but he does not give up.

He takes the first step, and then falls to the ground, but he doesn't give up. He gets up, and tries again till he gets it right. He is confident and determined, knowing he will eventually get it right. He doesn't let the noise around him distract him from his goal. He is not in competition with anyone but himself.

Somewhere between the infancy stage and adulthood, life

deals with us, causing us to lose our confidence. The noise and the competition out there distract us from reaching our goals, and achieving our dreams. We fail once, and fear to try again.

I want to be like a baby, not scared to give up. Yes, I may fall along the way, but I will get up, learn from my mistakes, and try again till I get it right.

If God put the dream in you, then it will happen, if only you do your own part. Persistence and hard work is the key to winning the game. Do not let the fear of failure stop you from achieving your dreams. Choose to be like the crawling baby who isn't afraid to try again.

ARE YOU A GOD-PLEASER OR PEOPLE-PLEASER?

Has God given you a vision or a dream, but you are hesitant about stepping out in faith because of the criticisms you may get from your loved ones or friends? Are you constantly worried about what people will say about you?

I was talking to one of my clients, and we discovered that the fear of criticism was the major factor preventing her from living her dreams.

The truth is that you can't please everyone. Someone will always have something to say about what you do or do not do. So why not stick with what God has called you to do?

For many years, I was scared to follow my dreams because of what my family, friends, or even strangers might say. Because of this, I stayed in my little corner, and continued doing what society expected of me, even though I was miserable and unfulfilled.

It all came to a boiling point one day, when I was pushed to the edge of the cliff, and I knew I had no other choice but to leap out in faith. Then my world changed. New opportunities came my way, I became fulfilled, several doors began to open for me, and I began to impact lives, to God's glory.

It took me a while, but I realised that people, especially loved ones, usually feel uncomfortable when you trying to rise above the level they are used to seeing you on. They see you as the girl you once were, and not the woman you are becoming. The truth is, you are changing, and change is usually hard to accept.

People would tell you it isn't possible, just because they cannot imagine you at a higher level. They may unconsciously, and sometimes, even consciously try to bring you down. You must not let them. The only person you should be aiming to please is God, because He put you here on earth, and KNOWS you. He gave you gifts and talents, which He wants you to use for His glory.

The people you are trying to please are just people, and they have their own issues and insecurities.

You should also be careful about the people you share your vision with. It is not everyone that can handle the greatness in you, so nurture your dreams quietly, and at the right time, all will be revealed.

Don't be scared to follow your dreams. Your focus should be on developing your gifts, and being a blessing to others. The vision God has given you is not about you only, it is beyond you, and to be used for HIS glory.

When you put this in mind, your focus will shift from being mindful of yourself to helping others, and what the critics have to say won't matter anymore.

If you want to SUCCEED, please God, and not man.

WILL-TRAINING - ATTITUDE ADJUSTMENT 101

You might agree with me that we live in a Me-centred world. Most people will only help others as long as it is convenient for them.

I remember that as a child, in Sunday school, we were taught that to have joy in our lives, we must put Jesus first, ourselves last, and others in between. We were even thought a song, using the Jingle Bells tune, to learn that Principle.

J-O-Y, J-O-Y,
This is what it means
Jesus first
Yourself Last
And Others In Between

As mothers seeking to be like Christ, we must emulate Him on living a selfless life. Even till the point of His death on the cross, He thought of others, and not of Himself.

Most people assume they do not have any control over their attitudes, moods, and emotions. This is not true. A lot of people believe this lie because they have not yielded themselves to the Holy Spirit for Will-Training. Do not forget that one of the fruit of the Spirit is self-control. We have control over what we think, how we feel, and how we behave. This is the major difference between us and other creations of God.

Let me take you on a journey of will-training by asking you to practice these basic activities, which I found a while ago.

- Smile when you'll rather frown
- Say a gentle word instead, when you want to snap
- Do a kind deed, however simple, even when it is not convenient
- Think a good thought when you'll rather not think at all
- See something beautiful in every disagreeable task
- Speak only good about those who come your way
- Deny yourself a little thing each day
- Be joyful, even in the face of sorrow and misfortune
- Give thanks to God, even for those things which try your soul

You can start by training yourself on the first task, i.e. Smile when you'll rather frown. Write it down on post-it notes and in your notebook. Think about it constantly, say it to yourself every morning when you wake up, asking for God's help, till it becomes stuck in your mind.

Acting it out might be difficult when you are in a bad mood, and there is clearly nothing to smile about. You might not feel like doing it, it might be forced, but just smile! You'll get better at it. You can also tell your friends and family about your attempt at will-training. That way, you would become accountable to them, and they can alert you when you are going off course.

After you master the first task, move on to the next one, till you have trained your will on every task. At the end of it all, I believe your attitude will improve exponentially. This might take a while, but I believe it will be worth your time.

You may find will-training very tough, but with God on your side, and determination in your heart, you will do it.

LAUGHTER IS THE BEST MEDICINE

Have you become so stiff and serious that you have forgotten how to laugh? Has life dealt with you so much that you have lost your sense of humour along the way? Are you sensitive to things people say to you? You need to learn to shake it off. Stop being so uptight. Smile a little!

When last did you laugh with your spouse and little ones?

If you observe your children carefully, you will find out that almost everything most likely cracks them up. I know they probably don't have responsibilities or cares, and can therefore afford to joke about. But think about it, you shouldn't have any cares in the world because God has already told you to cast all your cares on Him. Your being uptight is not going to change your situation. So yes, you CAN afford to laugh.

According to **helpguide.org**, here are a few good reasons why you should laugh some more:

- Laughter relaxes the whole body. A good, hearty laugh

relieves physical tension and stress, leaving your muscles relaxed for up to 45 minutes after.

- Laughter boosts the immune system. Laughter decreases stress hormones, and increases immune cells and infection-fighting antibodies, thus improving your resistance to disease.
- Laughter triggers the release of endorphins, the body's natural feel-good chemicals. Endorphins promote an overall sense of well-being, and can even temporarily relieve pain.
- Laughter protects the heart. Laughter improves the function of blood vessels, and increases blood flow, which can help protect against heart attacks and other cardiovascular problems.

Learn to laugh at yourself more than you currently do. Don't take yourself too seriously. Always find humour even in your problems. By doing so, you will transform your challenges into opportunities for creative learning.

Sometimes, when I make a blunder, I get really wound up, and want to give myself a knock, but I have since realised that when I joke about it to my husband or friends, and we laugh about it, the situation isn't always as bad as it seemed in the first place. I end up thinking of creative ways to correct my mistake, or I move on from it.

We know some events are clearly tragic, and do not warrant laughter. Nonetheless, most events in life don't carry a huge sense of either happiness or sadness. They fall into the grey zone of everyday life occurrences, where we choose to either laugh or lament about them.

Choose to laugh more from today. Start by smiling, even if there seems to be no reason to. Count your blessings; this will give you a reason to be happy. Hang out with positive people who like to have fun and laugh at themselves and life in general.

As you begin to laugh more, you will be more relaxed, attractive, and fun to hang out with.

YOU ARE A SUPER WORKING MUM BUT...

Yes, you are a Super Working Mum (SWM), but this doesn't mean you can do, or must do everything yourself. Most times, when you feel tired and overwhelmed, it is probably because you are stretching yourself too thin, trying to do all your tasks by yourself.

One secret of a SWM is, knowing when to ask for help. Even though you may finish tasks faster and do them better, you need to have a little faith in others. ASK for HELP! Asking for help doesn't make you less of a SWM.

Firstly, it is important that every day, you ask the ultimate giver of strength, GOD, for help. I don't know about you, but I certainly need a daily dosage of supernatural strength from above. You can also ask for help from your spouse, friends, siblings, co-workers, etc. when you need it. Be specific with your request when asking for help.

I remember that when I just delivered Professor J, taking my daughter, Bionic, to nursery became a struggle because Professor J was breastfeeding on demand, and we were still trying to establish a routine. Also, my husband had to go to work early by train, so he couldn't help with dropping her off. I initially thought I could manage lack of sleep, early breastfeeding, and nursery runs, but just thinking about it was overwhelming. I didn't have any other form of in-house help at the time.

Facing the prospect of juggling all these, I didn't even try to be a hero. On some mornings, I asked my husband to bath Bionic, and then asked my neighbour and friend if she could drop her off, since her son attended the same nursery. At first, I felt a bit awkward asking for help, but I noticed she was happy to help. That saved me a whole lot of stress and agony. The good thing is that she also knew I was available to help her whenever she needed it.

More often than not, your loved ones and friends are willing to be inconvenienced by you when you need help. Moreover, the worst they can do is say No. But if you don't ask, the answer will always be No.

So yes, you are super, but you can't do it all. Let others help you, and also be willing to help others. Whenever you are drowning, overwhelmed, or stressed, shout out if you need help.

EVERY SUPER WORKING MUM NEEDS A TO-DO LIST!

Using a to-do list is a simple but powerful way of staying organised, productive, and stress-free at work and home.

When all you do is think about the numerous tasks you need to complete, they usually feel much more overwhelming than they really are, and this may stress you out. Other times, you may forget what you need to do, miss deadlines, and then feel overwhelmed by the amount of work left for you to do.

If you write your tasks down, you would be able to stay focused, and minimise setbacks while being efficient and productive.

BENEFITS OF A TO-DO LIST

Some benefits of using a to-do list effectively are
- It helps you remember the important tasks you need to do
- It helps you avoid wasting time on frivolous tasks, so you can tackle important tasks first
- It enhances productivity

- It helps you stay focused and on top of your game
- It helps you stay organised and stress-free

HOW TO CREATE A TO-DO LIST

Taking some time to plan your day ahead will help you a great deal in being on top of your day. The traditional way of creating a to-do list is using a pen and a notepad. I believe the best time to create a to-do list is at night, before retiring to bed. Doing this helps you keep what you need to do the following day in mind. It also helps you feel energised, and become ready to start your day with a bang. If you prefer to, you could write out your list when you wake up in the morning.

On a sheet of paper, do a brain dump, and write all the tasks you need to complete. If these include large tasks, break them down into smaller sub tasks. You could get creative, and group your tasks into different categories such as work, home, shopping, etc.

Prioritise your tasks, and select the five most important tasks (MIT) you must complete that day.

According to Josh Kaufman, in his book, **The Personal MBA**, an MIT is a critical task that will create the most important results for your goals.

There is only so much you can do in one day, so it is wise to focus on the tasks that will move you closer to achieving your goals. Also by working on your MITs quickly, you'll have the rest of the day to handle anything else that comes up.

Once you have prioritised your list, transfer them to your notepad, arranging your tasks in descending order of priority. Once you have completed your five MITs, transfer the next set of tasks you want to complete. It may be a good idea to date your list.

USING YOUR TO-DO LIST

It is one thing to create a to-do list, but another thing to actually do what is on your list. There is no point creating a to-do list if you are not going to use it.

Start working your way through your five MITs. Once you finish a task, cross it off the list. You would most likely feel a sense of accomplishment when you tick off tasks as completed on your to-do list, knowing they are done and dusted. If you complete your five MITs, and you still have time, move on to other tasks on your list.

Review your list before you retire, and note how much you were able to accomplish. If you were not able to complete your to-do list for the day, don't worry about it. Pat yourself on the back for the tasks you completed, and simply transfer your uncompleted tasks to the next page, in addition to the tasks on your to-do list for the next day.

USING A SOFTWARE

In this technology-driven age, using a software or phone app to create your to-do list could even help you stay more productive. You can do much more with your to-do list when using a software, once you get the hang of it.

Most software can send you reminders about due tasks, connect dependencies between different tasks, and you can always update your list on the go. You can also share your work to-do list with team members, if you're collaborating on a project.

At a basic level, you can use Microsoft Excel or Outlook to manage your to-do lists. Some other online services are Toodledo, Todoist, and Cozi. I haven't tried any of them, but the reviews are satisfactory.

I don't like to complicate things, so I use Google calendar, which allows me to sync my laptop with my phone, with updates on my list. I also use the traditional pen and notepad method.

By adding this simple, yet powerful use of a to-do list to your daily life, you will realise that you would be more productive and less stressed. Try it, and see for yourself.

THE SECRET OF STAYING ON TRACK

You probably now have a to-do list you intend to tackle on a daily basis. However, when life gets in the way with one emergency or the other, there is a tendency for you to abandon your important tasks, to go putting out the daily fires that come your way.

Often times, most of what constitute emergencies or urgencies are things that could be

- Avoided, by making better choices upfront
- Deferred, by putting them off until it makes more sense to do them
- Refused, by saying "No, this just doesn't fit into what I want from my life right now"

Most mums complain about how there is so much to do, yet so little time. We complain about how the day just went by, but in most cases, we are the ones who let that happen.

How often do you start your day armed with your to-do list, only to realise at the end of the day, that you only tackled about two things on it? I know that happens to me sometimes.

The issue is that we cave in to distractions and interruptions, and later wonder where all the time went? Interruptions will definitely come, but you need to put a plan in place, to help you manage them.

It is one thing to set a big goal for our lives, but another thing to daily monitor if we are on or off track.

HOW CAN WE STAY ON TRACK?

First, figure out what your priorities are. Priority tasks are the things you do to make your goals happen. We dream of goals, but act on our priorities. Your true priorities are the tasks that get done first, and nothing should get in their way.

For example, you may say as a mother, your family is your highest priority, but when faced with a choice between working overtime for a promotion, or working sane hours so you can spend more time with your kids, you end up choosing one over the other, based on what is subconsciously more important to you.

On the other hand, we may find out that we end up doing other things that are not on our priority list. We might react to things rather than making conscious decisions on what we want to do, on a daily basis. These things we react to could be phone calls, emails, people, text messages, etc.

It's as if most of us have been conditioned to respond to interruptions with a sense of urgency, rather than thoughtful decisiveness. We suddenly give new tasks that come up a higher priority over what we were working on before.

DECISIVENESS vs. REACTION

Decisiveness says "it's important for me to stay on track of what I'm doing. I'll reply the person in 15 minutes." Reaction says "answer that email, someone needs something now," even if you are in the middle of something important.

There was a time when while I was getting some work done, I received a text message from a client who had issues with a job I had done for her organisation. My phone ringer is usually muted whenever I am working but somehow, I forgot to mute it on that particular day. As soon as the text message came in, my very initial thought was to drop what I was doing, and go solve the issue, but I took a deep breath, assessed the situation, and realised it wasn't critical. I decided it was best to deal with it after I reached the time limit I set for myself to complete my initial task. That way, I was able to stay on track.

Decisiveness is about telling incoming tasks to wait their turn, unless they are critically important enough to deserve your immediate attention.

A BIG TIME-STEALER

The mobile phone is one of the biggest time-stealers in this age. When the phone rings, we rush to answer it, a text message comes in, we hurry to address it, an alert from Facebook comes in, we get on Facebook, and then get off the track of what we were busy doing before. We all do it.

Would it be so bad to attend to missed phone calls later so you can stay on track? Will it harm you if you mute your phone ringer? Of course, if your business involves the use of the phone, this doesn't apply to you.

The flip side is that you have to find a balance when doing this, and not start ignoring people who need you. When you need to get your work done, put your phone away for that duration.

Please note that I am not advocating being rigid in your approach. I, for one, know that as a mother, unprecedented events come up, and interruptions will come in different shapes and sizes. When they do, ask yourself, "is this new thing worth getting off track from my current priorities?" This will help you make a judgment call as to what to do, and also allows you to be flexible, in case you need to deal with the new task immediately. It will also condition other people to respect your time, and ask "Is this a good time?" when they need you to deal with a situation.

The key point I want you to get from this is that you need to develop the habit of opposing reaction, so you can stick to your original priorities. You should change them only by making a conscious decision, when it is the right thing to do.

OUT OF MIND IS OUT OF SIGHT

Always have your to-do list in front of you, on a daily basis. They say out of sight is out of mind. Check the list three to five times a day to determine if you are still on track. By simply doing this, you will begin to make more conscious decisions during the day. Even if interruptions that require your immediate attention come, you will be able to get back on track once you have dealt with them.

If you want to master how stay on track, or regain control of your time, you can check out my online course, Take Back Control Of Your Time, where I cover practical strategies that will help you with time and self-management.

Scan this QR code using your smart phone or go to http://bit.ly/30-days-take-back-control to find out how take back control of your time

THE MYTH OF MULTITASKING

Multitasking is the act of engaging in two or more unrelated activities at the same time. A lot of women, especially mothers, pride themselves in their ability to multitask, as it gives them a sense of getting more done in less time. Several studies have however shown that multitasking can actually result in us wasting about 20 to 40 per cent of our time, depending on what we are trying to accomplish.

There are some menial tasks, which you can do at the same time, such as ironing and listening to an inspirational podcast or music, or cooking two different meals at the same time. However, when it comes to your life and business, it is a myth that multitasking would make you more productive and faster. In reality, multitasking slows you down, and leads to low performance and potentially costly errors.

You are better off focusing on one task at a time. In fact, your brain was designed to process one activity at a time. Your brain is not a glorified computer; even a computer has a limit to how much multi-processing it can do.

It is good to note that one thing your brain is extremely good at is rapidly switching from one task to another. MIT neuroscientist, Earl Miller, in an article[3] says, ***"Switching from task to task, you think you're actually paying attention to everything around you at the same time. But, you're actually not."*** What you are doing is moving from one task to the other at amazingly fast speeds. So in actual sense, we never multitask.

Imagine trying to talk to someone on the phone, and balancing your accounts at the same time. One or both of those tasks will suffer. Multitasking can reduce the quality of your work. It could also make you feel overwhelmed and stressed, as you are juggling several activities at the same time.

Whenever you multitask, notice how you feel when you are done. You probably feel tired, frustrated, and overwhelmed. Your brain most likely feels full and overloaded. On the other hand, notice how satisfied you feel whenever you devote your full attention to just one task at a time. You are able to focus, and probably finish it, knowing you've not only completed something, but also done your best at it.

To help you stay focused and get your work done, estimate how long it would take you to complete the task, set a timer for

[3]http://www.npr.org/templates/story/story.php?storyId=95256794

the estimated time, and focus solely on that task, blazing your way through it. When the timer goes off, give yourself permission to move on to the next task.

Get rid of all distractions. Turn off your phone ringer. Remove all visual and audible emails or social media alerts. If you find your mind wandering when you should be focusing on your work, you need to guide your thoughts back to the task at hand by putting yourself in the moment. Stay disciplined, Super Working Mum.

As a mum, you might feel there is so much to do, considering the different roles you play, but if you want to feel less-stressed, try handling one task at a time, or at least, unrelated tasks which you can combine. At first, this may seem difficult because you are probably used to multitasking, but you'll get there in the end.

If you want to move any aspect of your life to the next level, it is imperative that you ditch the act of multitasking, and stay focused on tasks that will result in growth.

ALL THINGS ARE POSSIBLE
TO HER WHO BELIEVES

When you pray, do you really believe your prayers will be answered? Does your faith quiver, or do you know God loves and wants the best for you?

When I was pregnant, I prayed for every single thing I wanted, including the delivery and the grace to cope with a new baby. I had read in books, and heard from people that I should expect sleepless nights, that babies confused their days with nights, and all kinds of scary stories.

I love a good night sleep, as you can probably tell by now, and I didn't see why having a baby should change that so I told God I wanted a baby who would sleep through the night.

From the very day we brought her home till she became a toddler, our daughter slept all through the night. There were very few occasions when she woke up to feed, but overall, our baby girl didn't disturb our sleep.

It was always funny when friends asked "how are you finding the sleepless nights?" and I would answer, "I don't know, I am sleeping well." They would then look at me in a weird manner, as if they didn't believe me. After a while, I stopped answering people, as they probably thought I was lying. Why anyone would lie about not having sleepless nights is beyond me.

When I was pregnant with my son, I asked God for a quick and easy birth, with no complications whatsoever. I also prayed I would have no tear because I had a tiny tear in the process of delivering my daughter. I prayed that everyone who would attend to me would be assigned specially by God himself.

The summary of my delivery experience is that I got what I prayed for. The only thing I forgot to pray for was no pain. My labour was very painful, but it only lasted for about three hours. I consider that quick, don't you? I didn't have any tear, and all the people who attended to me were lovely and very helpful. God came through for me! Overall, it was a good labour experience.

There are so many other examples in my life I can share, when God came through for me. Even when it seemed like He didn't, I knew He was still working everything out for my good.

What I want you to remember is that you must exercise your faith as the daughter of the Most High. Your story should be like the Hebrew women's story mentioned in the book of

Exodus. They had quick and easy labour, unlike the Egyptian women. The experiences in your life should be a supernatural one, and not similar to those in the world.

When you ask God for something in prayer, in the name of Jesus, stand on His word, believe it, and He will answer. He loves you, and wants the best for you. Simply believe.

ARE YOU SCARED OF COMPETITION?

There is no one else in the world like you. Your ideas might be similar to those of other people, but no one in the world has the exact combination of your gifts, abilities, experiences, trials, successes, strengths, and weaknesses - No single person. You therefore have a unique story to share with the world.

For you to be in competition with someone else, it means you must have the same vision. If God has given you a unique vision and purpose, then there is no need for competition.

Sometime ago, I was talking to a friend, and she said she admired what I was doing with Super Working Mum, but it was very similar to what God had laid in her heart to do. She therefore wanted my permission to continue with her project. While I perceived that to be a courteous gesture, I immediately told her she did not need my permission! I told her that though on the surface our ideas might look similar, they are totally different, because we have different experiences, ideas, and more importantly, different assignments from God.

When God gives you a vision, you do not need anyone's permission to do what He has called you to do. You can get inspiration from other people's assignments, but the way you will execute yours will be different. No two people can do the same thing the same way.

Don't be afraid to launch your business because someone else is doing something similar, or because you don't want competition. The truth of the matter is that there is no new idea in this world. It is the uniqueness you bring to the table that makes it different.

I like to use China Town as an example. There are loads of Chinese restaurants in China Town. They may all serve the same type of food, do a buffet from 10.00 a.m. till 2.00 p.m., and even have similar prices. However, each restaurant attracts its own set of customers due to different factors such as relationship built with customers, ambience of the restaurant, and customer service.

Are you afraid that someone will steal your genius idea, and copy what you are doing? First of all, there will be numerous copycats out there who will take your work, and copy it word for word. While this could be disheartening, knowing you have put in your hard work and sweat into what you do, I think you should be flattered that people are studying you, and want to copy you. That means they see you as a pacesetter and leader.

Secondly, this means you will always be ahead of them, because they have to keep waiting for you to make the next move before they can copy you. By the time they are catching up, you would have moved on to the next thing God is telling you to do.

So my dear SWM, there is nothing to be afraid of. If God has given you the vision, He will give you the wisdom and resources to accomplish it. The only person you should be in competition with is yourself. Your goal should be to strive to be better than the person you were yesterday.

As long as you do your work wholeheartedly, you are persistent, committed to serving your clients well, and building genuine relationships, you will succeed.

From this moment, I want you to stop focusing on the known and unknown competition, and concentrate on how to improve yourself. Then keep building your idea. Like Marie Forleo said *"The world needs that special gift that only you have."*

HOW TO SHINE LIKE A STAR IN THE SKY

Do you want to shine? Do you want to stand out? Do you want to be a light in this dark and crooked world? Then it is time to stop grumbling, finding faults, whining, and complaining.

"Do everything without grumbling or arguing, so that you may become blameless and pure, "children of God without fault in a warped and crooked generation." **Then you will shine among them like stars in the sky."** *Phil 2:14-15 (NIV, with emphasis)*

Whining or complaining is one of the things we don't like to see our children doing, yet we sometimes do it. What is that thing in your life you have been whining about? It is time to quit whining, and do something about it.

"I am not happy." Choose to be happy, you are in control, and responsible for your happiness. Think happy thoughts.
"I am always broke." Stop spending on the whim, and learn to save.
"I am fat." Lose the weight! Get a health coach; eat the right foods, and exercise.
"I am always tired." Stop engaging in unnecessary activities,

spread your tasks throughout the day, and plan ahead.
"I hate my job." Learn to love it, or find a new job.

… and the list goes on and on.

I know it is easier said than done, but the truth is the more you spend time complaining, the less in control you feel, and the more you feel stuck in that situation. Instead of feeling helpless, ask God to give you the strength to make the change you need to make today.

Ask yourself empowering questions, and not self-limiting questions. By doing this, you can change your outlook from one of lack to that of abundance and opportunities.

Switch from Why to How questions. Asking "Why?" limits your views, while asking "How?" or "What?" empowers you, and shows you there are possibilities. So instead of asking, "Why does this always happen to me?" ask yourself either, "What am I going to do about it?" or "How will I avoid this in the future?"

Make up your mind to make a change. Once it's settled in your mind, half the job is done. It is time to live a life of excellence, and not one full of constant complains.

My challenge to you is to pinpoint one issue you have been whining about, and come up with an empowering question that would force you to change your mind-set about that issue.

PUT ON YOUR GRATITUDE GLASSES

I once stumbled on the gratitude glasses (GG) concept initiated by The Joy Project[4]. The idea is for you to put on your gratitude glasses every morning, and not take them off till you go to sleep at night.

When you begin to feel sad, depressed, lonely, angry, or discontented, simply put on your gratitude glasses, and focus on things you are grateful for. Instead of whining and complaining about your work, husband, children, or whatever might be the source of discomfort, challenge yourself to put on your gratitude glasses instead, and say a word of gratitude.

Of course, it is much easier to be thankful when everything is going according to plan, and things are great in your life. The real test is in being thankful even when your situation seems hopeless. The mere fact that you are alive is enough reason to be grateful.

[4] http://www.thejoyproject.com/giant_gratitude_glasses

WHAT HAPPENS WHEN YOU PUT ON YOUR GRATITUDE GLASSES?

The challenges in your life turn to opportunities

You would begin to see life through the eyes of possibilities. Your financial crisis should be your opportunity to learn how to manage your finances better. The conflict in your marriage should be your chance to learn how to love deeply.

Your mistakes or failures become opportunities to learn

Wearing your GG has a tendency to make you realise you are doing the best you can at any point in time, based on the information you have. Instead of seeing the choices you make as mistakes, see them as an opportunity to learn and improve. Also, when others make mistakes, putting on your GG can enable you to be more lenient with them. They are only humans like you, after all.

You would welcome change

You would be more receptive to change when you put on your GG. You would stop trying to control life, become more excited about your future, and not worry when things don't go according to your plan. Your faith will be strong, and you would realise that everything is working out for your good.

Cultivate the habit of seeing life through your gratitude

glasses. When you do this, your thoughts would become more positive, and eventually reflect in your words and actions. You would begin to feel free and fulfilled!

No matter how bad things get, there is always something to be thankful for.

You may sometimes forget to put your GG on, but when you remember, don't beat yourself up. Just put them back on, and keep moving.

KEEP GROWING!

Gail Sheehy, an American author, journalist, and lecturer said, *"If we don't change, we won't grow, and if we don't grow, we're not really living."*

Even though you stop growing in height at a particular age, your spiritual, mental, and emotional growth is still in progress. You cannot afford to stop growing. You need to stay fresh, current, and on top of your game at work and home.

The fact that you are a mother, and busy raising your children is no excuse to stop your own self-development. Let your children know you can be mum, and still be relevant. Even if you are a stay-at-home mum, you can still grow if you choose to.

When you are committed to growth, you would not settle for ignorance, because the day you stop growing is the day you stop living.

Growth isn't easy; it involves hard work. It stretches you, and pushes you out of your comfort zone. It means leaving behind old habits, and adopting new ones that will propel you forward. Growth will cost you something, be it your time, money, or even friends.

Once you have committed to your own self-development, be aware that some people will try to stop you from growing. People generally enjoy playing safe. They feel uncomfortable around those who want to raise the bar. You can't blame them because they are probably trapped in a stagnant life, and don't know any better.

Your desire to change and grow above average would force those close to you to acknowledge their own habits, or how safe they are living their lives. Some would most likely see you as trying to be too good for the rest of the crew because you want to improve yourself.

When you decide to skip watching that television show to do something meaningful, expect some sneers from friends and family. When you decline the invitation to that party because you want to read a book, or work on a course that will help you progress in your career, expect whispers and discomfort. When you tell someone you can't talk right now, and will call them later, expect some discomfort and awkwardness.

Expect some resistance, but don't let that stop you. Don't

settle for less, and don't let people who refuse to grow stop you from growing. This is your life after all.

If the people around you are not pushing themselves or are indifferent to the bad habits in their lives, then hang out with those who also desire to grow. Help one another grow.

Will you remain stagnant or will you find ways to grow? Your growth is YOUR responsibility, and no one else's.

What steps are you going to take today to keep growing?

DEALING WITH CRITICISM GRACEFULLY

Nobody likes to be criticised. It can be demoralising when you put your heart and sweat into a project, then a colleague comes along, and pokes holes in it. Criticism can come in form of a stranger on Facebook writing hateful comments on your fan page, or a friend belittling your achievement when you are proud of attaining a goal you set for yourself.

The truth is, you will always be criticised, whether you like it or not. Once you step out of your comfort zone, people will offer you unsolicited advice about what you are doing, and how you are not doing it properly.

Sometimes, criticisms can be positive and constructive, other times, they can be downright hurtful, and even knock off your confidence. There is a popular saying that you can't control what people say, but you can control your reaction to them. This comes in handy when dealing with criticism. Since we cannot always avoid criticism, it is very important that we understand how to handle it gracefully when it comes.

Here are some ways that I deal with criticism gracefully, while still maintaining my dignity and confidence.

DON'T TAKE IT PERSONALLY

I have come to realise that most people form opinions based on their previous experiences, or the limited amount of information they have concerning any subject of discussion. As a result, they might judge you based on that premise. For example, your friend could be critical of a business idea you have, simply because she tried out a great idea once, and failed at it.

Knowing that your critic doesn't always see the full picture of your God-given vision, and your source of motivation, will help you depersonalise their words, and put their opinions in perspective.

ASK FOR SPECIFIC FEEDBACK

Imagine that after making a presentation, which you felt was successful; a colleague tells you "your points were quite hard to follow, you know?" Your first reaction may be to say something nasty, or say nothing, so your critic can leave you alone in peace. Instead of that, you can say something along the lines of, "oh, that's an interesting point of view. Please, could give me specific examples of what wasn't clear to you, and how you would have done it better?"

By doing this, you have shifted the focus back to the person. Your critic will either come up with a specific example, or stutter. If they are able to give you clear-cut feedback, thank them, and tell them you will take their comments on board. If they have no point to make, they would probably look silly, and never bother you again. On a lighter note, I suggest you try this tip only with peers, and not your boss.

FOCUS ON THE FACTS

When criticism is positive and helpful, it is much easier to see things from your critic's point of view. However, when the criticism seems demeaning, there is a natural tendency for you to get upset. But with some effort, you can turn it into an opportunity to learn.

When you are a bit calmer, reflect on what was said, and pick out the facts or truths. Write them down if you need to. This would help you stay focused and objective. Ignore everything else such as the tone, exaggeration, and patronising look. They are simply distractions. Dwelling on the negatives will not benefit to you in anyway, and will only knock down your confidence.

It might take a while to get over the hurtful remarks, but you will eventually get there. Don't suppress it; just let it float in your mind. Visualise yourself letting go.

GET A TRUSTED SECOND OPINION

Sometimes, criticism from certain people could be aggravating, and it may be difficult to see their points objectively. Try talking it over with someone you trust to be neutral enough to tell you the truth gently. Use them as a sounding board. Vent if you must.

Getting a second opinion will help you stick to the facts, and concentrate on what you need to change, if there is anything.

YOU CANNOT PLEASE EVERYONE

To be realistic, it is impossible to please everyone, so don't live in fear of what other people think. It is only their opinion after all.

Also, have you noticed that most times, people who pass cynical remarks are usually those sitting on the side lines, afraid to step out of their comfort zone? It is much easier for them to find faults with those who are trying to achieve their dreams, maybe out of annoyance or jealousy.

Ignore the naysayers and focus your energy on pursuing your goals. You getting feedback, be it good or bad, means people are noticing your efforts. I believe that's a good thing.

Dealing with criticism gracefully might take a while but keep at it, and get back on track each time you find yourself getting distracted by the noise. Your new way of thinking will also enable you to become more sensitive when giving feedback to others.

YOU NEED MORE OF
THIS TYPE OF STRESS!

Do you know that there is such a thing as good or positive stress? It is called Eustress (pronounced You-Stress), and was coined by endocrinologist Hans Selye. The prefix 'eu' is a Greek word which either means 'well' or 'good.' When used with the word stress, it means good stress.

Usually, when people talk about stress, they are most likely referring to negative stress, which is called distress. However, I believe that how you perceive a situation will determine the type of stress you feel, whether distress or eustress.

It is important to have Eustress in your life. Without it, you would become depressed, and most likely, feel like you are not living up to par. Eustress motivates and energises you to work on a task that may require some effort, or even prove challenging, but results in huge satisfaction.

For instance, some people get a buzz from skydiving, and experience eustress as a result. On the other hand, those who are scared of heights, like me, will find skydiving very distressing.

You need some level of eustress to achieve success in life.

SOME EXAMPLES OF EUSTRESS

- Acquiring new skills, especially when the development of that skill requires constant practice, e.g. learning how to drive, or learning to use a new software
- Networking and meeting new people to grow your business or client base
- Performing on stage, or taking part in a competition
- Preparing for big life events such as marriage, the birth of a new baby, or buying a house
- Studying for an intensive exam over a long period of time
- Investing in a romantic relationship with someone

It is also possible to feel distressed about the examples listed above. Our reaction to stimulus, our attitude, and how in-control we feel about a situation determines whether we will feel eustress or distress.

HOW TO SWITCH FROM DISTRESS TO EUSTRESS

Change your attitude

Begin to see the stress-triggers in your life as challenges, rather than threats. When you adopt this mentality, it would be easier to think more positively about an issue, and how to tackle it.

When you see a situation as a threat, you will feel distressed about it. This can affect your physical and mental health. However if you see the situation as a challenge, you will be on the lookout for ways to tackle it, and your excitement will be pumped up, which gets you looking for solutions.

Engage in Positive Thinking

When negative thoughts cross your mind, make a conscious effort to keep them at bay, breathe, and then replace them with positive ones. Meditate on scriptures to keep your mind from wandering about. By simply seeing the positive perspective of a situation, you can avoid being distressed.

Change self-limiting statements to empowering questions

Statements like "this is impossible" or "I can't do it" should no longer be part of your vocabulary. If you find yourself making such statements, ask yourself, "how can I handle this?" or "how can I make this possible?" You will be surprised at creative solutions you come up with.

Maintain a sense of humour

Many of us take life too seriously, which results in distress.

Smiling and laughing are powerful expressions we all need to make, in order to have a balanced life. Studies show that having a smile on your face can release endorphins, which makes you feel better, and can eventually become happier.

Ask yourself "in a year or two from now, will this even matter?" This will help you put the situation in proper perspective, and realise that stressful situations will always pass.

Eustress motivates you to keep moving forward with an activity or project, even though you might find it demanding and challenging. It also helps to promote emotional balance and confidence.

Remember that not all types of stress are bad. Stress is simply the body's response to changes that create challenging demands. It is how you perceive the situation that matters. So whatever situation you may find yourself in, applying the tips listed above will help you experience more eustress in your life.

LIVING WITH LESS

I was raised by my parents to make do with what I have, and to differentiate between a want and a need. It didn't matter if everyone at school was wearing or using something, if it wasn't a need, you were not getting it!

It was easier in the twentieth century and before then, but now, it seems the message of 'having it all, when I want it' is being ingrained in our subconscious, and in the minds of our children. Many people are caught up in measuring one another's worth by what they wear, where they live, the car they drive, etc. Many people are envious of one another, and are busy acquiring and storing treasures on earth, rather than in heaven.

In the parable of the rich fool, the man who had made lots of money, and wanted to enjoy it all by himself, Jesus warns us to beware of greed and covetousness. Life is not measured by what you have, but what you do with it.

One of your goals as a Super Working Mum should be being content with what you have, not jealous of what others own, and not bothering about piling earthly possessions. It is about teaching our children the value of contentment, and living a clutter-free life.

I must confess that I am a recovering hoarder. I keep thinking I will need this or that in future, so I hardly get rid of old things. However, these days, I am being conscious about my clutter, and getting rid of them gradually. I have realised that clutter can actually have a negative effect on my wellbeing.

Do this simple test. Which room do you feel more peaceful in, one that is cluttered and filled with junk, or one that is airy, with no clutter?

Remember the 80-20 rule we discussed earlier in the book. We tend to wear 20% of our clothes and shoes 80% of the time. 80% of your clothes are most likely just gathering dust in your wardrobe. It might seem traumatic giving out 80% of your clothes, but I believe you won't even notice their absence when they are gone. The recipient will feel blessed and happy to receive the clothes you no longer need.

To be honest, the uncluttering process is overwhelming for me, but I am taking it one drawer at a time, one room at a time. With these baby steps, I am well on my way to becoming clutter-free!

Is your identity tied to what you own, your job, status, position, or accolades? If yes, you need to do an identity check. Your identity should be in Christ. Remember you came to this earth with no possessions, and will leave with none.

When we live with less, it helps us to stop thinking about ourselves, but focus on being a blessing to others. It also helps us to teach our children to be content, live a life of giving, and not measure success by other people's possessions, or compare their lives with others.

A SIMPLE SECRET GUIDE
TO REMEMBERING BIRTHDAYS

Are you awful at remembering birthdays of friends, family, colleagues, and clients? Do you only remember someone's birthday when Facebook alerts you? If yes, what then happens to those who are not on Facebook? You would most likely forget their special days.

How do you feel when people remember your birthday? I guess you feel special. I do too!

I know we are all busy saving the world, juggling the balls of life, extinguishing fires, and being super mums, but we should not forget simple things in life, such as birthdays of loved ones.

At a young age, I learnt from my mum that remembering people's birthdays is a kind thing to do. She is great at it, and never forgets birthdays of friends, family members, in-laws, church members, etc. She will either call you, or send you a text message on your birthday. Everyone who knows her knows her for this.

I am not an expert like her, but I always smile when I notice people are delighted because I remembered their birthdays.

Do you want to stop sucking at remembering birthdays? Then let me share a very simple way of ALWAYS remembering with you. No, this does not involve using Facebook, or an app. In fact, you will be surprised at the ease.

Before the advent of mobile phones, I had a small calendar booklet where I noted down the birthdays of my family and friends. I looked at it every day, to check if someone's birthday was approaching. If it was, I would send the celebrant a card or a message to wish him or her happy birthday. People always wondered how I remembered, and were always delighted that I did.

In recent years, Facebook has taken over, and a lot of us rely on it to remind us of birthdays. If you are my friend on Facebook, you might have noticed my birthday is not there. It may seem cheeky, but that's because I expect people who care about me to remember my birthday without the assistance of Facebook.

I know there are other apps or tools out there that help with remembering birthdays, but trust me; you don't need any fancy apps. Let's keep it simple, shall we?

Surprisingly enough, you already have the tool you need. It is your phone. I believe every mobile phone has a reminder feature or calendar.

All you need to do is note someone's birthday once. As soon as you know it, get your phone, go to your calendar, click 'add new event', and type in "xxx's birthday." Different phones may have different settings. Set a reminder alert. That is not all. Look for "Repeat" or "Repeat Event" and change that to "Yearly". Make sure "End Repeat" is set to "Never". Click "Done", and that is it. For as long as you have that phone, you will never forget a birthday again.

Once your phone reminds you of someone's birthday, don't ignore it, take action. Send them a message, an e-card, a card, or an email to wish them happy birthday. I guarantee you that your friend, loved one, or client will feel special because you remembered, especially if they don't have their birthday on Facebook for one reason or the other.

Some of us are good with remembering birthdays by heart, but sometimes life gets in the way, and you may forget. By setting a reminder on your phone, it is almost guaranteed that you will remember.

This simple secret does not only apply to birthdays, but anniversaries and other special or important dates. Try it from today, and observe the reaction you get from others. Remembering other people's birthdays is part of what makes you super, and most of all, loving.

LET THEM SAY

I was talking to one of my clients during a business strategy call, and she said one of the things stopping her from moving forward with her business idea was because of what people might say or think. She wasn't sure if people would be enthusiastic about her idea.

Her statement made me realise that there are many others who feel this way. I have also felt that way before, letting the assumed thoughts of others stop me from actualising my dreams.

First of all, you are not psychic, so there is no way you can know what others are thinking about you unless they tell you. Secondly, most people are thinking about themselves, and not you. Thirdly, it does not matter what others think.

It is astonishing to realise how much emphasis we place on what other people think about us. These are people who change their minds easily, and have their own insecurities, issues, and challenges.

The only approval you should be seeking is that of God. He is the one who created you, and His thoughts towards you are of good, and not of evil. He knows you best; He has bestowed gifts upon you, and established a destiny that is full of success for you.

People will always have an opinion about you, and talk about you, no matter what you do. Let them say! What matters is what God says. If you have an idea you are passionate about, step out of your comfort zone, and do something about it. Don't wait for the approval of others before you take action. In fact, approval may never come, so don't let that be a determining factor in achieving your dreams. Not everyone will like what you do; some may even judge you. Sometimes, you might walk the journey alone for a long time. The path to success isn't always laced with commendation and recognition, but it will be worth it in the end.

Your gift will make room for you on earth; you will stand before personalities that matter. You will impact lives, to God's glory. Most importantly, when you leave this earth, you would have done the will of the Father, and He will welcome you with opened arms saying, "Well done, good and faithful servant."

So like I did to my client that day, I want to encourage you as well. Follow your passion, do your best, and don't wait for anyone to give you credit for it. Don't wait for others to be enthusiastic about what you do. All of that will come later.

Just remember that God is cheering you on, and only His approval matters.

PROCRASTINATION IS
THE THIEF OF TIME

Procrastination is something everyone has experienced in life. It is important to know how to deal with it, as it could have a dire impact on your success in life if you do not tackle it head on.

According to Joseph Ferrari, a professor of psychology at DePaul University in Chicago, and author of Still Procrastinating: The No Regret Guide to Getting It Done, around 20 per cent of U.S. adults are chronic procrastinators.

It is usually much easier and convenient to engage in light-hearted matters than to focus on work, business, school, paying that bill, etc.

WHY DO YOU PROCRASTINATE?

According to Tuckman, Abry, and Smith[6], there are 15 key reasons why people procrastinate.

1. Not knowing what needs to be done
2. Not knowing how to do something

Tuckman, B.W., Abry, D.A, & Smith, D.R. (2008). Learning and motivation strategies: Your guide to success (2nd ed.). Upper Saddle River, NJ: Pearson Prentice Hall

3. Not wanting to do something
4. Not caring if it gets done or not
5. Not caring when something gets done
6. Not feeling in the mood to do it
7. Being in the habit of waiting until the last minute
8. Believing that you work better under pressure
9. Thinking that you can finish it at the last minute
10. Lacking the initiative to get started
11. Forgetting
12. Blaming sickness or poor health
13. Waiting for the right moment
14. Needing time to think about the task
15. Delaying one task in favour of working on another

Can you identify with any of these excuses above? I sure can!

WHAT ARE THE EFFECTS OF PROCRASTINATION?

Procrastination can have a negative impact on your health, as you may begin to feel stressed and ill when deadlines at work suddenly approach, or you realise you have so much to do, and so little time to do it.

It could also affect your relationships, as your family, friends, or clients might not be able to rely on you to come through for them at the right time, if you keep missing appointments or deadlines.

HOW TO DEAL WITH PROCRASTINATION

Do a brain-dump

Sometimes just thinking about the numerous tasks you have to complete could prevent you from actually doing anything on your list, thus leading to procrastination.

Do a brain-dump, and write down everything you need to do. Then classify the tasks you have written down under the following four categories.

1. What tasks do you need to do that will take you closer to your goals? Remember your work-life vision.
2. What tasks can you delegate?
3. What tasks can you do later?
4. What tasks can you get rid of because they are not necessary, and just taking up space in your head?

Focus on the tasks that fall under the first category, and create a prioritised to-do list. Delegate the tasks in the second category. Park the tasks in the third, and forget about the ones in the fourth category. This will give you more clarity, and even motivate you to get some work done, now that you have sorted your brain-dump.

Break complex tasks into smaller manageable tasks

When a task seems complex, you could feel intimidated by it. Determine what smaller steps you need to take, in order to enable you complete that huge task. For example, if you are planning a family event, what things do you need to do, and by when? What resources do you need? Write them down.

Once you outline the process and the smaller tasks you need to complete, it would be easier to work on the smaller tasks, bit by bit, in order of priority.

Get rid of the "Right frame of mind" myth

Sometimes, you might tell yourself you have to be in the right frame of mind before you work on a project or a task. That happens to me sometimes as well. However, I have come to realise that once I actually begin a task, I eventually find myself in the right frame of mind. I only needed to start!

If you keep waiting to be in the right mood before you work, it may never come, and you will never get anything done. Like Nike says, JUST DO IT.

Get rid of distractions

Distraction is a very good friend of procrastination. Some days, you might realise you spent most of your time dealing with distractions and interruptions, as opposed to accomplishing your tasks.

TV, emails, mobile phones, social media, i.e. Facebook, Twitter, Pinterest, Google Plus, Instagram, etc. can get in our way, if we allow them to. This is where discipline and focus comes in.

Set an alarm, and assign some time to focus on some quality work. Turn off the ringer of your phone, turn off social media/internet, and turn off the TV if you work from home. Yes, you can do it! Tell yourself you will not be distracted till you finish the task at hand.

It can be hard, but practice makes perfect. With time, you will be great at eliminating distractions, and dealing with procrastination.

Reward Yourself
Once you have completed your task during your allocated time for work, it is important to reward yourself with something fun you enjoy doing. Personally, when I have accomplished my tasks, I sometimes reward myself with catching up on a TV programme I like. You could take regular five to ten minutes breaks during the day to catch up on emails, social media, or returning phone calls.

Change Your Mind-set

Dealing with procrastination involves you changing your mind set about your priorities, and how you view the use of your time. It may seem like no big deal, but by procrastinating, you gradually lose out on success.

It may not be easy to totally eradicate procrastination, but knowing the reasons why you procrastinate could help you deal with it more effectively.

Remember, procrastination is the thief of time.

ARE YOU EASILY OFFENDED?

I remember that as a teenager, I used to be very sensitive, and easily get offended because of what people said or did to me. I used to get very worked up, and I held grudges. I was always defensive, moody, and had a snarl on my face. Most people knew I didn't stand for nonsense, and that I was 'hard-core'.

What a hard, negative, and miserable life is one full of offences. Offence is something you have to guard against. Holding on to anger and offences can affect your spiritual and emotional health. It is a trick the devil uses as bait to lure us into miserable lives of bitterness, resentment, unforgiveness, and even hatred.

People who are easily offended are:
· **Selfish**- get offended when they don't get their way
· **Negative**- believe the worst of everyone else, and are always finding faults
· **Insecure**- feel rejected when things don't go according to plan, or when people say No to them
· **Miserable**- are unhappy and depressed
· **An easy target of Satan,** who in fact, is their real

enemy. When you don't forgive others, you are making it easy for the devil to have a foothold in your life

- **Hindering God's plan for their lives**. God can't lift you high if there is unforgiveness in your heart
- **Not free, and have no joy.** When you are offended, you won't have peace of mind

Does this reflect your life? Are you holding on to offence? Do you need to forgive someone today?

"Holding a grudge is like letting someone live rent-free in your head." - Unknown

Harbouring offence, bitterness, and resentment does nothing good for you. It only harms you, and can have a negative impact on your health. Most times, the other party does not even realise they have hurt you.

Offence hinders you from connecting with your heavenly father. It also stops your prayers from getting answered. In fact, you will not be able to pray or worship God when you are angry with someone else.

Studies have shown that unforgiveness and bitterness can be the root cause of deadly diseases such as heart attacks, high blood pressure, headaches, and chronic pain. Just do a

Google search on forgiveness in relation to health, and you will be astonished at your findings.

When you forgive others, it is not usually for them but for yourself, because you set yourself free.

I know forgiving can sometimes be hard. Some people have done the uttermost painful unforgivable things to us, but the reward of forgiveness is much bigger than what you get when you hold on to the offence.

Some people are so full of offence that every time you have a conversation with them, they only talk about what this person said two years ago, or what that person did last week. They go on and on about how they have been mistreated. Who wants to be around such negativity? Not me!

Learn not to be too sensitive. When people say things that offend you, don't commit it to heart. Don't mediate on it, and rehash it in your mind.

If you find it hard to forgive others or even yourself, ask God to help you. He will. Ask Him to fill your heart with His love. Pray for the person who offended you. By praying for them, you will take your mind off the offence, and feel better for it. You will also be putting the devil to shame, and letting him know he has no power over you.

Today, through the power of God, I am no longer that miserable angry teenage girl. I have learnt to take things easy, and accept people with their idiosyncrasies because I know I have mine. I am now more tolerant towards people. When I find it hard to shake off an offence, I simply pray for that person and the situation. My life is peaceful now.

Be determined to live a life without offence.

BY THE FLESH OR THE SPIRIT?

One question I always ask myself is "how have I been living my life, according to the flesh or the Spirit?"

The bible says: *For those who live according to the **flesh** set their minds on the **things of the flesh**, but those who live according to the **Spirit**, the **things of the Spirit**. For to be carnally minded is death, but to be spiritually minded is life and peace. Rom8: 5-6 (NKJV, with emphasis).*

This means that when you live according to the flesh, you typically think about

"What I want out of my life."
"What I can accomplish with my life."
"What I can gain out of this."

The above thought pattern leads to spiritual death because your focus is on yourself, and not on Christ.

On the other hand, when you live according to the Spirit, you generally think about

"What God wants for my life."
"What God can accomplish through my life."
"How much I need the Lord."
"How great the Lord is."

The result of this is eternal life and peace, because you are focused on Him, and know it is about Him.

The truth is that the flesh vs. spirit choice is an important one every believer faces daily, as those are the only two ways to handle issues of life. Many times, I think about what I want, and not what God wants. I think about my heart's desires, not God's heart desires. I need to get past thinking of ME, to thinking of what my Father desires. I need to get past spending time on my affairs, to spending time on God's affairs. I need to start living according to the Spirit!

How then do I do that? I need to ask God daily for supernatural power to renounce the path of the flesh. I need to feed my Spirit, by feasting on God's word, putting my expectations and cares on Him, and focusing on Him. This will enable His Spirit to bring forth fruit such as love, joy, peace, long suffering, kindness, goodness, faithfulness, gentleness, self-control, in me, which will bring glory to His name.

So how do you live, by the flesh or by the Spirit?

LIVING FOR CHRIST

I once read somewhere that life is not a dress rehearsal. You have only one life to live until you are either called home by God or Christ returns. Since this is the case, your goal should be to live your life to God's glory, in preparation for heaven.

This world is just a journey, not our final destination. Heaven is! By living for Christ on earth, we would begin to experience God's best for our lives.

In order to live above mediocrity, succeed on this earth, and also be prepared for Christ's coming or life after death, I encourage you to imbibe these habits.

- Personally know and experience God's **love**.
- Know and experience God's **purpose** for you.
- Intentionally and passionately **act** on your purpose **daily**.

KNOW AND EXPERIENCE GOD'S LOVE FOR YOU

God loves you, Super Working Mum. That is a fact. The

scripture testifies to God's love for you. He sent His only son Jesus to die for you, and redeem you from sin and death, according to John 3:16. All you need to do to accept God's love is acknowledge that you are a sinner, believe that Jesus died for you, and confess Him as your Lord and saviour. If you are yet to do this, there is a prayer you can say, written at the back of the book.

It is one thing to know God loves you, but another thing to actually experience His love. Some people believe God's love is determined by their behaviour or performance. God's love does not work that way. He loves us with an unconditional love, and nothing can separate us from His love, according to Romans 8:39.

There is nothing more or less that you can do that will make God love you more or less than He already does. All He wants is for you to experience His love daily, no matter your circumstance.

You can experience God's love daily by
- Spending time in prayer
- Reading and meditating on His Word
- Worshiping Him, to experience His presence
- Thanking Him for His goodness in your life

Sometimes the guilt of sin can stop you from experiencing and enjoying God's presence. We are not perfect, and God knows this. According to Psalm 51:17, all He desires from you is a broken and repentant heart, so when you fall into sin, claim His forgiveness. His mercy is bigger than your sin.

KNOW AND EXPERIENCE GOD'S PURPOSE FOR YOU

"Before I formed you in the womb I knew you, before you were born I set you apart; I appointed you as a prophet to the nations." Jer 1:5 (NIV)

You were not born by chance. Your parents may not have intended to have you, but God had a solid plan for you when you were conceived. You were placed on earth for a purpose. Do you know that purpose? If you are not sure, look deep into your life and prayerfully think about the gifts and talents God has given you, those things you do effortlessly, or that come second nature to you. God has given every single person on earth one or more talents.

You can also ask those around you to tell you what they believe your strengths are, because your gifts may be more obvious to people around you than to you.

Do not envy other people's gifts. Why become an imitation of someone else when you can be the original of yourself? Don't you know you are a Limited Edition?

Once you have discovered your gifts, ask yourself "how can I use my gifts and talents for God's Kingdom?" At home and work, or with strangers, how can you use your gifts to be a blessing to others?

DELIBERATELY AND PASSIONATELY ACT DAILY, ON YOUR PURPOSE

"Let your light so shine before men, that they may see your good works and glorify your Father in heaven." Matt 5:16 (NKJV)

Your purpose is usually tied to your talents, and should be used to bring glory to God. Your talents are not just for your personal gains. Once you know your purpose, find ways to work on them and strengthen them. Everything you do on a daily basis should be in line with the purpose God has called you to.

Complacency can be the enemy of progress. Step out of your comfort zone, in faith, and observe how God will use you in ways you could never have imagined. Through you and your purpose, people will come to know God, His love, and the saving power of His son, Jesus Christ.

Live your life as if today is your last day on earth. When you live purposefully on earth for His glory, God will reward you on earth, but more importantly, in heaven.

Fear, anxiety, lack of motivation, or stress of life may try to side-track you from living intentionally for Christ. If this is your case, ask God to give you the grace and strength to live for Him… only Him.

Jesus is coming back. Will you be ready when He does?

CONCLUSION

I hope this book has blessed you. My hope is that every Super Working Mum who picks and reads this book knows Jesus Christ personally.

Since I gave my life to Christ and walk daily with Him, my life has been transformed. I have seen evidence of His grace, love and power in my life- both in good and bad times.

We can only live a supernatural life through God's power, and you can only have access to this power by having a personal relationship with Him.

Having a personal relationship with God is as simple as ABC.

Accept that you are a sinner, and ask for God's forgiveness
Believe in Jesus, and put your trust in Him
Confess that Jesus is your Lord.

The Bible promises that when you sincerely ask God for forgiveness, and trust in Jesus, you will experience new life in Christ. *"... If you confess with your mouth the Lord Jesus and believe in your heart that God has raised Him from the dead, you will be saved." Rom 10:9 (NKJV).*

With all your heart, surrender your life to Jesus Christ. Confess your sins. Ask God to forgive you. Believe in His son, Jesus, and thank Him for the gift of everlasting life.

To express your repentance and commitment to a new way of life, say a simple prayer to God. There is no special formula. Just pray using your own words. Pray from your heart to God, and believe He has saved you. If you feel lost, and just don't know what to pray, here's a prayer of salvation you can recite.

"Father, I understand I have sinned against you. Please forgive me. Wash me clean. I promise to trust in Jesus, Your Son. I believe He died for me; He took my sin upon Himself when He died on the cross. I believe He was raised from the dead.

"Thank You, Father, for your gift of forgiveness and eternal life. From this day forward, Lord, I give you control of my life. Make me a new person, and help me to live for You, in Jesus' name, Amen."

You are now part of God's family. I rejoice with you! Your final step is to receive the free gift of forgiveness and eternal life.

The Bible says *"Yet to all who received him, to those who believed in his name, he gave the right to become children of God." John 1:12 (NIV).*

When you receive Christ into your heart, you become a child of God. You have the privilege of talking to Him in prayer any time you want, and about anything.

Get a Bible, and begin to study it to grow in your Christian faith. I suggest you start with reading the gospels of Matthew, Mark, Luke and John. Join a Bible-believing church, as you will need support from other believers that can encourage you in your new faith.

God loves you, Super Working Mum. Accept His love for you today, and trust in Him. As you relate to God, and live according to His guidance, your life will change.

If you have backslidden, and not living for God, but for yourself, know that your Heavenly Father cares about you, and wants you to return to Him. If you draw near to Him, He will draw near to you. You can say this prayer of rededication.

"Dear Lord Jesus, I believe you died on the Cross for me, and you were raised from the dead. I confess you as my Lord. I repent of my sins, both known and unknown, and I ask you

to forgive me. Open my blinded eyes, that I might see and know you and myself better.

"Heavenly father, I rededicate myself to your path in life, of faith, of love, of fellowship and service to my fellow man. I yield myself to you. I commit myself to bringing forth the fruit of the spirit: love, joy, peace, longsuffering, gentleness, goodness, faith, meekness, and temperance. I renounce and turn from the fruit of the flesh, because I belong to you. I give myself to you fully, and ask you to please come in and take control of my life. In Jesus Name, I pray. Amen."

Congrats Super Working Mum, for making things right with God. To show your commitment, start spending time with God every day. Study the Bible, and pray. Ask God to increase your faith and understanding of the Bible. Hang out with other Christians in church and bible study groups, which could also be on the internet.

God bless you!

note from the Author

Thank you for buying this book. I would love this book to be read by as many working mums as possible, because I believe they would benefit from it.

If you enjoyed reading it, you can please help spread the word by doing the following:

Recommend it. Suggest this book to other working mums, or buy it as a gift for someone.

Talk about it. Mention it on Facebook, Twitter, or Google Plus. Create a conversation about it using *#swmbook*. You can write about it, or review it on your blog. You may also use the cover image as your profile picture on social networking sites.

Review it. Leave a review online. It's very easy to leave reviews on Amazon.

Many thanks for helping me spread the word.

Other books by Aloted Omoba:

Boosting Your Confidence, 15 Steps to Success In the WorkPlace

about The Author

Adetola Amure, who goes by the pseudonym Aloted Omoba, is passionate about the empowerment of women, especially mothers. She is also an inspirational writer.

She has a first degree in Computer Science from the University of Botswana, and a Masters in Operational Research from Lancaster University, UK.

For some years, she worked in the Management Consulting and Telecoms industry, with top organisations like Accenture and British Sky Broadcasting, as a Business Analyst. However, after two children, and by divine guidance, she now spends her time helping Christian working mums who are overwhelmed create profitable businesses around their families, so that they can live a more fulfilled and balanced life.

A finalist in the Yes I can Award category of the 2014 Inspirational Women's Award, she is a go-getter, and believes she can do all things through Christ. Her first eBook, Boosting Your Confidence, 15 steps to success in the workplace, was well received by working mothers.

She lives in Essex, United Kingdom with her loving husband Tj and two children.

You can interact with Aloted online via
Website: www.superworkingmum.com
Facebook: www.facebook.com/SuperWorkingMum
Twitter: www.twitter.com/SuperWorkingMum

11866164R00117

Printed in Great Britain
by Amazon.co.uk, Ltd.,
Marston Gate.